Survival ot the Fireflies

A Univocal Book

Drew Burk, Consulting Editor

Univocal Publishing was founded by Jason Wagner and Drew Burk as an independent publishing house specializing in artisanal editions and translations of texts spanning the areas of cultural theory, media archaeology, continental philosophy, aesthetics, anthropology, and more. In May 2017, Univocal ceased operations as an independent publishing house and became a series with its publishing partner, the University of Minnesota Press.

Univocal authors include:

Miguel Abensour
Judith Balso
Jean Baudrillard
Philippe Beck
Simon Critchley
Fernand Deligny
Jacques Derrida
Vinciane Despret
Georges Didi-Huberman
Jean Epstein
Vilém Flusser
Barbara Glowczewski
Évelyne Grossman
Félix Guattari
David Lapoujade
François Laruelle

David Link
Sylvère Lotringer
Jean Malaurie
Michael Marder
Quentin Meillassoux
Friedrich Nietzsche
Peter Pál Pelbart
Jacques Rancière
Lionel Ruffel
Michel Serres
Gilbert Simondon
Étienne Souriau
Isabelle Stengers
Eugene Thacker
Siegfried Zielinski

Survival of the Fireflies

Georges Didi-Huberman

Translated by Lia Swope Mitchell

A Univocal Book

University of Minnesota Press
Minneapolis · London

This work received support from the French Ministry of Foreign Affairs and the Cultural Services of the French Embassy in the United States through their publishing assistance program.

The University of Minnesota Press acknowledges the contribution of Jason Wagner, Univocal's publisher, in making this volume possible.

Originally published in French as *Survivances des lucioles,* copyright 2009 by Les Éditions de Minuit, 7, rue Bernard-Palissy, 75006 Paris.

Cover art: *Vagalumes,* October, 2008. Copyright Renata Siqueira Bueno.

Published by the University of Minnesota Press
111 Third Avenue South, Suite 290
Minneapolis, MN 55401-2520
http://www.upress.umn.edu

ISBN 978-1-5179-0574-3 (pb)

A Cataloging-in-Publication record for this book is available from the Library of Congress.

Printed in the United States of America on acid-free paper

The University of Minnesota is an equal-opportunity educator and employer.

22 21 20 19 18   10 9 8 7 6 5 4 3 2 1

Contents

1. Hells?

The great heavenly light *(luce)* versus small lights *(lucciole)* in the infernal bolgia of evil counselors. — Dante inverted in the period of modern warfare. — In 1941, a young man discovers flashes of desire and innocence in fireflies. — A political question: Pier Paolo Pasolini in 1975, neofascism and the disappearance of fireflies. — The people, their resistance, their survival, destroyed by a new dictatorship. — Hell made real? The Pasolinian apocalypse today: reproached, approached, experienced, expanded.

2. Survivals

Have the fireflies *all* disappeared, or might they survive *in spite of all*? Denis Roche's poetico-visual experience of intermittence: reappearing, redisappearing. — Minor lights: deterritorialized, political, collective. Pasolini's political and sexual despair. No living community without a phenomenology of its presentation: the luminous gestures of fireflies. — Walter Benjamin and dialectical images. Every means of imagining is a means of politics. Politics of survivals: Aby Warburg and Ernesto De

3. Apocalypses?

Interrogating the contemporary through paradigms and a philosophical archaeology: Giorgio Agamben with Pasolini. — The "destruction of experience": apocalypse, grief for infancy. Between destruction and redemption. — Derrida's critique of the apocalytic tone in philosophy, and Adorno's unthought of the resurrection. — In a theory of survivals, there is neither radical destruction nor final redemption. Image versus horizon.

4. Peoples

Lights of power versus lights of counterforces: Carl Schmitt versus Benjamin. Agamben beyond any distinction. — Totalitarianism and democracy according to Agamben, via Schmitt and Guy Debord: from acclamation

1

Hells?

Well before he described the great light of Paradise shining out in all its eschatological glory, Dante decided to reserve a quiet but significant fate, in the twenty-sixth canto of the *Inferno*, for the "tiny light" of those glowing worms, the fireflies. The poet is observing the eighth bolgia of hell, a political bolgia if ever there was one, since we can recognize a few eminent citizens of Florence gathered there, among others, all under the same condemnation as evil counselors. The entire space is scattered—constellated, infested—with small flames that look like fireflies, just like those that people see in the countryside on fine summer nights, flitting here and there, on the whim of their quiet, passing, intermittent wonder:

> As many fireflies (in the season when
> the one who lights the world hides his face least,
> in the hour when the flies yield to mosquitoes)
>
> as the peasant on the hillside at his ease
> sees, flickering in the valley down below,
> where perhaps he gathers grapes or tills the soil—
>
> with just so many flames all the eighth bolgia
> shone brilliantly, as I became aware.[1]

In Paradise, the great light beams out in sublime concentric circles: a cosmic light in glorious expansion. Here, though, the *lucciole* wander feebly—as if a light could whimper—in a sort of dark pocket, that pocket of sins made so that "each [flame] steals its sinner" *(ogne fiamma un peccatore invola)*.[2] Here the great light does not shine; there are only shadows, where the "evil counselors" and corrupt politicians crackle faintly. In his famous drawings for *The Divine Comedy,* Sandro Botticelli includes minuscule faces, grimacing and imploring within languid spirals of infernal sparks. But because he halts before plunging all of this in shadow, the artist fails to represent the *lucciole* as Dante describes them: the white vellum is only a neutral background where the "fireflies" stand out in black: dry, immobile, and absurd outlines.[3]

In any case, this is the miserable "glory" of the damned: not the brilliance of well-earned celestial joys but rather the small, painful glimmer of wrongs, dragging along under accusations and punishments without end. Like the opposite of moths consumed in the ecstatic instant of their contact with flame, these glowing worms of hell are poor "flies of fire"—*fireflies,* as the French *lucioles* are called in English—who bear within their very bodies an eternal, tormenting burn. Pliny the Elder was once troubled by a sort of fly, called *pyrallis* or *pyrausta,* that could fly only in the fire: "So long as it remains in the fire it will live, but if it comes out and flies a little distance from it, it will instantly die."[4] Suddenly the lives of fireflies seem foreign, troubling, as if made from the surviving matter—luminescent but pale, weak, often greenish—of ghosts. Faint flames or lost souls. No surprise that one may suspect, in the uncertain flight of fireflies in the night, something like a meeting of miniature phantoms, strange beings whose intentions may or may not be good.[5]

The story I want to sketch out—the question I want to construct—begins in Bologna, in the last days of January or the first days of

February 1941. A young man, nineteen years old, registered at the College of Literature, discovers all of modern poetry, from Hölderlin to Giuseppe Ungaretti and Eugenio Montale, along with Freudian psychoanalysis and existentialist philosophy. He doesn't forget his Dante, of course. But now he rereads *The Divine Comedy* with fresh eyes: less for the compositional perfection of the great poem than for its labyrinthine variety; less for the beauty and unity of its language than for the exuberance of its forms, its twists, its appeals to dialect, to slang, to wordplay, to intersections; less for its imagination of celestial entities than for its descriptions of earthly things and human passions. Less, then, for its great *luce* than for its innumerable and erratic *lucciole*.

That student is Pier Paolo Pasolini. If he goes back to Dante now for a reading—a rereading that will never cease—it's in large part because of his discovery of Erich Auerbach's history of literary mimesis, as set forth in the masterful essay *Dante: Poet of the Secular World.*[6] If Pasolini reimagines the human *Commedia* beyond schoolroom teachings and Tuscan nationalism, this is also because of those "figurative flashes," as he later writes, that he experiences in Roberto Longhi's seminars on the "primitive" painters of Florence, from Giotto to Masaccio and Masolino. The great art historian contrasts Masaccio's whole humanist vision, such as his use of cast shadows, with Dante's many reflections on the human shadow and the divine light.[7] But even in this period of triumphant fascism, when speaking to his students, Longhi does not omit much more contemporary—and more political—shadows and lights, such as those found in Jean Renoir's *The Grand Illusion* or Charlie Chaplin's *The Great Dictator.* Apart from all that, the young Pier Paolo plays *attaccante* (striker) for the university soccer team, which will emerge victorious that year from its intercollegiate championship match.[8]

Apart from all that—though very nearby—the war is raging. The dictators are talking: on January 19, 1941, Benito Mussolini meets Hitler at the Berghof; then, on February 12, he tries to convince General Franco to take an active role in the global conflict. On January 24, British troops begin their recapture of East Africa, held by the Italians: the British occupy Benghazi on February 6, while the Free French Army embarks on its campaign in Libya. On February 8, the English fleet bombards the port of Genoa. These are the days and nights of late January 1941. Let's imagine something like a complete inversion of the relationship between *luce* and *lucciole*. On one side, propagandist spotlights halo the fascist dictator in a blinding light. But the powerful spotlights of antiaircraft defenses, too, are chasing the enemy though the shadows of the sky, in "chase scenes"—as they're called in the theater—as watchtowers hunt the enemy through the darkness of the camps. This is a time when the "evil counselors" are in their full and luminous glory, while resistants of all kinds, active or "passive," transform into fireflies, fleeing to make themselves as secret as possible even as they continue to send out their signals. So Dante's universe is completely inverted: now, hell is out in the daylight, with its corrupt politicians glorious and overexposed. As for the *lucciole,* they're trying to escape as best they can, from the threat, from the condemnation that, from now on, will crush their existence.

This is the context in which Pasolini writes a letter to his boyhood friend Franco Farolfi, between January 31 and February 1, 1941. Small stories in the larger history. Stories of bodies and desires, stories of souls and private doubts in the larger confusion, the century's larger turmoil. "I am marvelously idiotic—but in the way the gestures of someone who has won the lottery are idiotic—at least the stomach-ache is beginning to go away, and so I feel myself prey to euphoria."[9] Already, then, there are both prey (in Italian, *preda*; for example, one says *preda di guerra* for the "spoils of war") and euphoria. Already there is that pincer movement, with its painful combination of law and desire, guilt and transgression, accepted anguish and controlled pleasure: small lights of life, with their heavy shadows and their painful forced consequences. Which is what the very next lines in Pasolini's letter to his friend show. The young humanist mentions what he calls the *parténai*—from the Greek word *parthenos,* indicating virginity—writing,

> As for virginities I pass long hours of languor and extremely vague dreams which I alternate with mean, stupid attempts at action and with periods of extreme indifference. Three days ago Pariah and I went down to the den of a merry prostitute where the big tits and the breath of naked forty-year-olds made us think with nostalgia of the lidos of innocent child-hood. Then we peed dejectedly.[10]

Words from a young man deep in shadow, seeking his way through *la selva oscura* and the moving glimmers and flashes of desire (*lucciola,* in Italian slang, designates the prostitute but also that mysterious feminine presence in the old movie theaters that Pasolini no doubt visited often: the "usherette" armed with her little flashlight to guide the spectator among the rows of seats in the dark). Between euphoria and prey, pleasure and error, dreams and despair, this young man waits for a light to appear, at least the trace of a *lucciola,* if not the kingdom of *luce.* And that is exactly what happens (and even justifies the story). Love and friendship, passions that for Pasolini were absolutely linked, are suddenly embodied in the night, in the form of a cloud of fireflies:

> Friendship is a very nice thing. The night I am telling you about we ate at Paderno and then in the complete darkness

we climbed up towards Pieve del Pino—we saw an immense number of fireflies which made clumps of fire among the clumps of bushes and we envied them because they loved each other, because they were seeking each other with amorous flights and lights while we were arid and all males in artificial peregrinations.

Then I thought how beautiful friendship is and the bands of twenty year old youths who laugh with their innocent male voices and take no notice of the world around them, continuing along their lives, filling the night with their shouts. Theirs is a potential masculinity. Everything in them turns to laughter, to bursts of laughter. Never does their virile enthusiasm appear so clear and overwhelming as when they seem to have become once more innocent children because their complete and joyous youth is still present in their bodies.[11]

Here, then, are the *lucciole,* raised up as impersonal lyrical bodies for that *joi d'amor* the troubadours sang about so long ago. Plunged in the great guilty night, men sometimes let their desires shine out, let out their shouts of joy, their laughter, like so many *flashes of innocence.* No doubt, in the situation Pasolini describes, there is a sort of breakdown relative to heterosexual desire (since fireflies are male and female, lighting up to call to each other and calling to each other to copulate, to reproduce). But what remains essential, in the comparison established between flashes of animal desire and bursts of laughter or shouts of human friendship, is that innocent and powerful joy that appears as an alternative in these times of triumphant fascism, whether too dark or too well lit. Pasolini even indicates, very specifically, that art and poetry also offer such flashes, at once erotic, joyous, and inventive. "[It's the same] when they are talking about Art or Poetry," he says of these luminous young people and their "virile enthusiasm" in the midst of the night. "I have seen—and I saw myself in the same way—young men talking about Cézanne and it seemed as if they were talking about one of their love affairs, with a shining and troubled look."[12]

Pasolini's letter ends and culminates with the violent contrast between this *exception* of innocent joy, which receives and radiates the light of desire, and the *rule* of a guilt-ridden reality, a world of terror that materializes here as the interrogating rays of two spotlights and the terrifying barks of guard dogs in the night:

> That is how we were that night—we clambered up the sides of the hills among the undergrowth which was dead and their death seemed alive, we made our way through orchards and trees laden with black cherries and reached the top of a high hill. From there one could see two very distinct and fierce searchlights very far off—mechanical eyes from which there was no escape, and then we were seized by terror at being discovered while dogs barked and we felt guilty and fled along the brow, the crest of the hill. Then we found another grassy patch—a circle so small that six pines a little apart were sufficient to encompass it. There we lay down wrapped in blankets and talking pleasantly together we heard the wind beating and raging in the woods and we did not know where we were nor what places were around us. At the first signs of light (which is something unutterably beautiful) we drank the last drop from our bottles of wine. The sun was like a green pearl. I stripped off my clothes and danced in honour of the light—I was all white, while the others wrapped up in their blankets like *peones* [Spanish peasants] trembled in the wind.[13]

One could say that, in this final scene, Pasolini strips naked *as a worm,* affirming at once his animal humility—close to the soil, the earth, the vegetation—and the beauty of his young body. But, "all white" in the brilliance of the rising sun, he dances *like a glowing worm,* like a firefly or a "green pearl." An erratic glimmer, certainly, but a living glimmer, the flash of desire and poetry incarnate. Pasolini's entire body of literary, cinematographic, and political work seems to be shot through with such moments of exception, moments in which human beings become fireflies—luminescent beings, dancing, erratic, elusive, and *resistant* as they are—before our amazed eyes. The examples are innumerable: one has only to think of Ninetto Davoli's aimless dance in *The Sequence of the Paper Flower* in 1968, the young man's luminous grace standing out against a busy Roman street, and even more against the haunting background of some of the darkest images in history: bombardments intercut with antiaircraft spotlights, "glorious" visions of corrupt politicians juxtaposed with the war's somber mass graves. In the end, we know, the firefly-man will be crushed under an absurd divine judgment:

> Innocence is a sin, innocence is a sin [you understand?]. And the innocents will be punished because they no longer have the right to be innocent. I cannot forgive those who walk through injustice, war, horror and chaos with a happy smile of innocence on their face. There are millions of innocents like you all over the world who want to disappear from history rather than shed their innocence. And I have to kill them even if I know they can't help it. I damn them like the barren fig tree. Die, die, die.[14]

Of this celestial condemnation, sweet Ninetto clearly understands nothing. He just asks, more innocently than ever, "What?" before crumpling in a position that exactly reproduces a cadaver in films from the Vietnam War. The firefly is dead, its movement and light lost in the political history of our dark moment, which condemns its innocence to death.

The question of fireflies, then, is political and historical before all else. In his article on Pasolinian politics, which does not fail to mention Pasolini's 1941 letter, Jean-Paul Cunier is correct in saying that the Bolognese youth's innocent beauty is no "simple question of aesthetics and discursive form, [for its] stakes are enormous. It is a matter of separating political thought from its discursive matrix" and, in this way, arriving at that crucial place where the political becomes incarnate, in the body, movements, and desires of each person.[15] It goes without saying—not only because Pasolini repeated it for years but also because we can have this experience every day—that the *fireflies' dance,* this moment of grace that resists in the world of terror, is the most fleeting, the most fragile thing there is. But Pasolini, followed by a number of his commentators, went even further: he actually theorized, or affirmed as a historical thesis, the *fireflies' disappearance.*

February 1, 1975—that is, thirty-four years to the day, or rather to the night, after his beautiful letter on the fireflies' appearance, and exactly nine months before he was brutally murdered in the dead of night on the beach in Ostia—Pasolini publishes an article in the *Corriere della sera* newspaper about the political situation of the time. The text is titled *Il vuoto del potere in Italia,* but it would later be republished in the *Scritti corsari* under the soon-to-be famous title *L'articulo delle lucciole,* "The fireflies article."[16] Yet I would argue that this is, above all, the *death notice* for the fireflies. It consists of a funeral lament on the moment, in Italy, of the disappearance of fireflies, those human signals of innocence annihilated by the night—or by the "fierce" brilliance of spotlights—of triumphant fascism.

The thesis is this: it's a mistake to believe that the fascism of the 1930s and 1940s was defeated. Mussolini was executed, of course—hanged by his feet in the Plaza Loreto in Milan in an "infamous" staging, characteristic of Italy's oldest political customs.[17] But from the ruins of that fascism, another fascism was born, a new terror that, in Pasolini's view, was even deeper and more devastating. On one hand, "the democratic-Christian regime was the pure and simple continuation of the Fascist regime"; on the other hand, "something" happened in the middle of the 1960s, "something" that made way for the emergence of a "radically, totally, and unforeseeably new type of fascism."[18] The first phase of the process was marked by "police violence and disregard for the constitution," all of it drenched in "atrocious, stupid and repressive State conformity," against which "intellectuals and opposition of this period cherished ridiculous illusions" of political reversal.[19]

The second phase of this historical process began, according to Pasolini, at the very moment that "the most advanced and critical intellectuals did not realize that 'the fireflies were disappearing.'"[20] In the words that this polemicist—or rather provocateur, as Pasolini is usually called—brings together, all his violence is assembled, *constructed [montée]* with all the care of the poet. The polemicist does not hesitate to speak of "genocide," justifying his choice on this occasion with a reference to Karl Marx, on the bourgeoisie crushing the proletariat.[21] As for the poet, he deploys the ancient, lyrical, and delicate—that is, the autobiographical—image of fireflies:

> At the beginning of the sixties, the fireflies began to disappear in our nation, due to pollution of the air, and the azure rivers and limpid canals, above all in the countryside. This was a stunning and searing phenomenon. There were no fireflies left after a few years. Today this is a somewhat poignant recollection of the past.[22]

The return to this poetico-ecological image is not in any sense an attempt to soften the violence of the phenomenon that Pasolini is diagnosing. Rather, it's a way to insist on the anthropological dimension—in his eyes, the most profound and radical dimension—of the political process in question. Pasolini uses the hyperbolic word *genocide* in this period to designate more precisely a general movement of *cultural decay,* which he clarifies frequently with the expression "cultural genocide." The idea that a deeper fascism had supplanted Mussolinian gestures appears clearly in 1969, in Pasolini's interviews with Jean Duflot.[23] Later, in a 1973 article titled "Acculturation and Acculturation," the filmmaker explains his idea: in the time of historical fascism, it was still possible to resist—that is, to light up the darkness with a few glimmers of thought, by rereading Dante's *Inferno,* for example, but also by discovering dialect poetry or, very simply, by observing the fireflies' dance in Bologna in 1941. "Fascism proposed a model, a reactionary and monumental model, but it remained a dead end. Various individual cultures (peasants, workers, the subproletariat) continued undisturbed in identifying with their models, for repression was limited to obtaining their adherence in words. In our day, however, adherence to the models that the center imposes is total and unconditional. We reject true cultural models. The renunciation is complete."[24]

In 1974, Pasolini fully develops his theme of "cultural genocide." The "true fascism," he says, is one that takes over the values, the souls, the languages, the gestures, the bodies of the people.[25] It's that which "leads, without executions or mass killings, to the suppression of large portions of society itself," which is why this genocide must be called "that [total] assimilation of the quality and the way of life of the bourgeoisie."[26] In 1975, just as he writes his text on the fireflies' disappearance, the filmmaker has also taken up the motif—the tragic and apocalyptic motif—of the *disappearance of the human* at the heart of contemporary society: "All I want is that you look around and take notice of the tragedy. What is the tragedy? It's that there are no longer any human beings; there are only some strange machines that bump up against each other."[27]

It's necessary to understand that the improbable, minuscule

splendor of fireflies, in Pasolini's eyes—eyes skilled in the con-
templation of a face or the selection of just the right movements
of his friends' and actors' bodies—is a metaphor for nothing
other than humanity in its essence, humanity reduced to the
simplest of its powers: to send us a sign in the night. Does Pasolini see, then, his contemporary environment as a night that
would finally devour, subjugate, or *reduce the differences* formed
in darkness by those luminous flashes of fireflies in search of
love? This last image, I believe, is not yet quite right. It's not
actually into the night that the fireflies have disappeared. When
the night is darkest, we're capable of seizing on the faintest
glimmer, and even the expiration of light remains visible to
us in its *trace,* however tenuous. No, the fireflies disappeared
in the blinding glare of the "fierce" spotlights: spotlights from
watchtowers, on political talk shows, in sports stadiums, on
television screens. As for those "strange machines that bump
up against each other," they're nothing but the overexposed
bodies, with their stereotypes of desire, that confront each
other in the bright light of sitcoms—so very distant from the
quiet, the hesitant, the innocent fireflies, those "memories of
the past, not without pain."

In his text on fireflies, Pasolini's protest inextricably blends the
aesthetic and political, if not the economical, aspects of this
"void of power" that he observes in contemporary society, this
overexposed power of the void and of indifference, all transformed
into commodities. "I could see with 'my senses,'" he says, to
give an empirical, sensorial, and even poetic character to his
analysis, "how the power of a consumption-based society mod-
eled and deformed the conscience of the Italian people, finally
arriving at an irreversible degradation."[28] The truly tragic and
harrowing character of such a protest comes from the fact that
Pasolini found himself forced, in these last years of his life, to

renounce the very thing that had constituted the source of all his poetic, cinematographic, and political energy.

That source was his love of the people, which markedly transforms Pasolini's narratives of the 1950s and all his films from the 1960s. It flows through his poetic adoption of regional dialects,[29] the foregrounding of the subproletariat in works such as *Stories from the City of God* or *The Long Road of Sand*,[30] the depiction of suburban poverty in films like *Accattone*—contemporary, by the way, to Franz Fanon's *The Wretched of the Earth*—*Mamma Roma* or *La Ricotta*.[31] In his theoretical essays, on the other hand, Pasolini tries to show the specific power of popular cultures in order to recognize the true capacity of historical, thus political, *resistance,* of their anthropological work of *survival*: "Slang, tattoos, laws of silence, mannerisms, social structures and the entire system of relations with power remain unaltered," he says, for example, regarding Neapolitan culture. "Even the revolutionary era of consumption—that which has radically changed the relations between a centralized culture belonging to power and working-class cultures—has only left the Neapolitan working-class culture a little more isolated."[32]

One day, when asked whether, as an artist of the Left, he felt nostalgic for the times of Bertolt Brecht or French "engaged" literature, Pasolini responded in these terms: "No! My nostalgia [is] for those poor and real people who struggled to defeat the landlord without becoming that landlord."[33] An anarchist way, it seems, of disconnecting political resistance from a simple party organization. A way of conceiving emancipation differently than through a single model of accession to wealth and power. A way of considering memory—slang, tattoos, mannerisms belonging to a given population—and thus the desire that comes with it, as so many political powers, as so many protests, capable of reconfiguring the future. This involved a certain "mythification" of the working class, of course. But in his view, the myth—what

Pasolini often called the "power of the past" and what can be seen at work in films like *Oedipus Rex* and *Medea*—was actually a part of the revolutionary energy belonging to the poor, to the *degraded* people of the usual political game.[34]

For this is what is doomed, in the "disappearance of fireflies," to failure and despair. In the image of fireflies, Pasolini sees a whole reality of working-class people in the process of disappearing. If "the language of things changed" in a catastrophic way, as the filmmaker says in his *Lutheran Letters*, it is primarily because "the spirit of the people disappeared."[35] And we could say that here we have a question of light, a question of *apparition*. Thus the significance, the rightness of his appeal to fireflies. From this perspective, Pasolini seems to follow in the footsteps of Walter Benjamin and in the zones of reflection, closer to him, explored by Guy Debord.

Benjamin, we recall, articulates his entire political theory beginning with an argument on the reciprocal apparition and *presentation* of peoples and of powers. "*The crisis of democracy can be understood as a crisis in the conditions governing the public presentation of politicians,*" he writes in 1935, in his famous essay "The Work of Art in the Age of Its Technological Reproducibility."[36] As to the "society of the spectacle" that Guy Debord attacked, it arises with the *unification* of a world "basking in the perpetual warmth of its own glory," whether that glory is a generalized negation and *separation* between "living human beings" and their own capacity to appear otherwise than under the domination—the raw, cruel, fierce light—of the commodity.[37] Beginning in 1958 in a text titled "Televisual Neo-Capitalism," Pasolini had already determined the extent to which the light of the small screen was destroying exposition itself and, along with it, the dignity of the working classes: "[television] not only does not attempt to elevate the cultural level of the lower layers, but provokes in them an almost agonizing inferiority."[38]

This is why "there are no longer any human beings," no more fireflies either, in our cities as in the country. This is why, in that final year of 1975, the filmmaker must "renounce" his *Trilogy of Life* and, in a manner, "suicide" his own love of the people in a few extremely violent lines in "Disappearance of the Fireflies":

> Perhaps the only precedent to the Italian trauma produced by the clash between pluralist archaism and industrial equalization was pre-Hitler Germany. In that country also, the values of different specific cultures were destroyed by the violent recognition process of industrialization, with the consequence of producing those gigantic hordes who had neither the ancient peasant or artisan roots or not even a modern bourgeois background, and who made up the savage, abnormal and unpredictable bodies of Nazi troops.
>
> Something similar is now occurring in Italy, with even greater violence in that the industrialization of the sixties and seventies was also a decisive mutation compared to that in Germany fifty years ago. As we all know, we are not now facing a new age, but rather a new era of human history, with human history seen in periods of one thousand years. The Italian people could not have behaved worse than they did in confronting this historic trauma. Over a period of several years they have become, especially in the Center-South, a degenerate, ridiculous, monstrous, and criminal population—one need only go into the street to understand this. Of course, in order to understand the changes in people, you have to understand the people themselves. To my detriment, I liked them, the Italian population, both outside of the power systems—in fact in desperate opposition to them—and outside of populist and humanitarian systems. I felt real love for them, rooted in my personality.[39]

A love now uprooted, annihilated, exterminated. "I would give all of Montedison ... for a firefly," Pasolini concludes.[40] But the fireflies have disappeared in this time of industrial and consumerist dictatorship, when each and every person ends up *exhibiting himself* like a product in a window—a way, precisely, of *not appearing*. A way of bartering civil dignity for the infinite profits of the spectacle. The spotlights have invaded the entire social space; no longer will anyone escape their "fierce mechanical eyes." And worst of all, everyone seems happy, believing he can "make himself beautiful again" by taking advantage of this triumphant industry of political exhibition.

Hell. Doesn't all this sound like the description of a nightmare? Yet Pasolini insists on telling us: this is really reality, *our contemporary reality,* this political reality so obvious that nobody wants to see it for what it is but that the "senses" of the poet, the seer, the prophet, receive so powerfully. The brutality of Pasolini's language is equaled only by the delicacy of his perception, confronted by an infinitely more brutal reality. But are cries and lamentations—"The fireflies are dead!"—the only response to this reality? Beyond the hypersensitive "senses" of the poet, we understand that such a description also implies "sense" or meaning: the very significance, not only literary but also philosophical, of what the word "hell" could mean, a few centuries after Dante. In his political texts and until his final film, *Salò,* Pasolini tried to present and represent to us that new reality of the circle of "frauds" or the bolgia of "evil counselors," not to mention the "luxurious," the "violent," and other "falsifiers." What he describes as a fascist domain is thus a *hell made real,* from which nothing can escape, to which we are all now condemned. Guilty or innocent, no matter: damned in every case. God is dead; the "frauds" and "evil counselors" have taken advantage of his absence to claim his throne of Supreme Judgment. From now on, they're the ones who decide the end time.

The doomsayers, the prophets of misery, are delirious and

demoralizing in the eyes of some, fascinating visionaries in the eyes of others. It's easy to *reprove* Pasolini's tone, his apocalyptic accents, his exaggerations and hyperbole, his provocations. But how can we not *prove* vulnerable [*éprouver*] to his nagging fear when everything in Italy today—to speak only of Italy— everything seems to correspond more and more exactly to the rebellious filmmaker's infernal description? This is why a commentator on Pasolini may *approve* of that description, to the point of paraphrase, to the point of overkill: "Then doubtless yes: this world is fascist and it is more so than the previous, because it is total regimentation even of the depths of the soul; it is more so than any other, because it no longer leaves any possible exteriority to a domain of despotism without limits, without direction and without control. . . . Today . . . this characteristic, now exorbitant in its power in the time of market totalitarianism, is so widely assimilated that artistic production is primarily a merciless competition for the chance to get recuperated."[41]

Said another way—by another of his attentive readers— the "disaster" that Pasolini diagnoses would be described as "infinitely more advanced than was supposed by the process that inspired the three films from the early 70s [*The Trilogy of Life*]. In fact, in 1975 it is no longer possible to oppose 'innocent bodies' to cultural and commercial massification, to the trivialization of all reality, for the very good reason that the culture industry has taken hold of bodies, of sex, of desire, and injected them into the consumerist machine. The illusion of the refuge of memory, of the buoy of resistance stuck in the deep straits of popular culture, is dissolved. The more or less pagan lines of flight drawn in the films composing the *Trilogy* are cut off, and it's as if there were no longer any margins or external limits to the territory of consumption; consumption is a *power*, a machine whose energy endlessly absorbs its own negativity and reabsorbs, without interruption or rest, even that which claims to oppose it."[42]

The fireflies have disappeared, which means the *culture,* in which Pasolini had until then recognized a practice—whether a folk practice or an avant-garde one—of *resistance,* has itself become a tool of totalitarian barbarity, confined as it is now within the commodified, prostitutional domain of generalized *tolerance*; "Pasolini's prophecy—realized—finally comes down to one phrase: culture is not what protects us from barbarity and what must be protected from barbarity; culture is the very space in which the new barbarity's intelligent forms flourish. Pasolini's argument is very different from that of Adorno and his followers, who thought that it was necessary to defend high culture and avant-garde art against mass culture; the *Scritti corsari* are rather a manifesto, arguing for the defense of political spaces, political forms (debate, polemics, struggle) against cultural homogenization. Against the general regime of *cultural tolerance.*"[43]

Here, then, is Pasolini proved, approved, extended, out-done. The apocalypse continues apace. Our current "civilization and its discontents" is heading in this direction, it seems, and most often, this is the way we experience it. But it's one thing to point out the totalitarian machine and another to concede its total and definitive victory so quickly. Is the world so totally enslaved as our current "evil counselors" dream—as they plan, program, and try to convince us—that it is? To postulate this is, in fact, to give credence to what the machine tries to make us believe. To see nothing but the black night or the blinding glare of spotlights. To act defeated: to be convinced that the machine is finishing its work without rest or resistance. To see only the *whole.* And thus not to see the space—though it may be interstitial, intermittent, nomadic, improbably located—of openings, of possibilities, of flashes, *in spite of all.*

The question is crucial and no doubt complex. So there will be no dogmatic answer to this question, by which I mean, no general, radical, *total* answer. There will only be signs, singularities, fragments—brief, weakly luminous flashes. Fireflies, to use our current expression. But what have they become today, those light signals that Pasolini announced in 1941 and then sadly renounced in 1975? What are their chances of apparition or their zones of erasure; what are their powers, their fragilities? What *part* of reality—as opposed to a whole—can the image of fireflies address today?

2

Survivals

But first, have the fireflies truly disappeared? Have they *all* disappeared? Do they still emit—but from where?—their wondrous intermittent signals? Do they still seek each other out somewhere, speak to each other, love each other in spite of all, *in spite of all* the machine—in spite of the murky night, in spite of the fierce spotlights? In 1982, a work actually titled *The Disappearance of Fireflies* appeared in France. In it, the author, Denis Roche, describes his experiences as a poet and photographer.[1] Obviously the title echoes, in homage, Pasolini the poet and filmmaker, murdered seven years earlier. Denis Roche gives one chapter of his book the form of a letter—a style that Pasolini himself had used often—addressed to Roland Barthes; and from beyond Barthes's death, Roche delivers a firm yet gentle reproach that, in his *Camera Lucida,* Barthes omits all that photography could set in motion in the areas of "style," of "freedom," and, he says, of "intermittence."[2]

At first this pattern of intermittence seems surprising (but only if one thinks of photography as an object rather than an act). In reality, it is fundamental. How can we not think here about the "flashing" nature of Walter Benjamin's dialectical image, a concept intended precisely to understand the way in which *epochs become visible,* how history itself can appear to us as a brief flash that must be named an "image"?[3] The intermittence of the image-flash leads us back to the fireflies, of course: a passing, fragile pulse of light. Seven years after Pasolini's death, did the fireflies still make the epoch visible? The title that Denis Roche gives his text would seem to say no. However, at a certain moment in our reading, everything changes. The general theme sketched out within this critique of Barthes suddenly gives way to a journal fragment, written on July 3, 1981, in an Italian village. Just as in Pasolini's 1941 letter, here is an innocent stroll among friends, through the countryside after nightfall. And here, too, is the *reappearance,* the magical discovery, of fireflies: "At least twenty of them are moving around in the brush. We're all exclaiming to each other . . . each of us talking about when and where we'd seen them before." A beauty so incredible, yet so modest: "Two more are flying along a little farther, two little alternating dashes of Morse code glowing below the embankments." A stunning beauty, stunning "to see that, at least one more time in life."[4] In a moment, though, "the last fireflies go away, or they purely and simply disappear."[5] And the chapter of wonder closes. *Redisappearance* of fireflies.

But how have the fireflies here disappeared or "redisappeared"? It's only from our view that they "purely and simply disappear." It would be far more correct to say that they "go away," purely and simply. That they "disappear" only insofar as the viewer chooses not to follow them. They disappear from the viewer's sight because the viewer remains in place, which is no longer the right place to see fireflies. Although elsewhere in his book, Denis Roche himself provides all the elements for understanding this relationship, through the photographic necessity of making an image—which Barthes did not mention, immobilized as he was, faced with the grief of the "this-has-been"—using an *intermittent lighting* that, as with fireflies, is also the vocation of *lighting in motion*. Photographers are first and foremost travelers, Roche explains: moving around

like insects with their large, light-sensitive eyes. They form "a
troop of fireflies on the alert. Fireflies busy with their intermittent lighting, flying at low altitude over the troubled hearts and
spirits of our times. Soft clicks of wandering fireflies, brief little
lights . . . with the addition of a motor that makes this attentive
gaze into a psalmody of light, click clack, light, click clack, etc."[6]

I myself lived in Rome a decade after Pasolini's death. Even
then there was, at a certain spot on the Pincian Hill—a place
called the "Bamboo Forest"—a veritable community of fireflies whose lights and sensual movements, that slow, insis-
tent manifestation of desire, fascinated everyone who passed
through there. Today I'm amazed that I never thought to take
any photographs of them (if only just to try). In any case, the
fireflies had not disappeared between 1984 and 1986, even in
Rome, even in the urban heart of centralized power. They were
still surviving quite well in the early 1990s. They must have
been there a long time, since a score for piano, dating from
the first World War, is still kept in the Casadésus Archives at
the French National Library, with the title *Les Lucioles de la Villa
Médicis.*[7] More recently, I noticed with sadness that the Pincian
Bamboo Forest has been cut down. So the fireflies have, once
again, disappeared.

There is probably every reason for pessimism about the
Roman fireflies. At the very moment that I write these lines,
Silvio Berlusconi is preening away in the spotlights; the North-
ern League is taking action and the Romani people are getting
kicked around, all the better to kick them out. There is every
reason for pessimism, but it's more necessary than ever to
open our eyes in the night, to move around without rest, to
set out again in search of fireflies. I've learned that there are
still two thousand known species of these little bugs (class: In-
secta; order: Coleoptera; family: Lampyridae[8]) living throughout
the world. Certainly, as Pasolini noted, water pollution in the

countryside is killing them, and air pollution in the city as well. We know also that artificial lighting—streetlights, spotlights—considerably disturbs the lives of fireflies, as it disturbs the lives of all nocturnal species. In extreme cases, this can lead to suicidal behavior, for example, when firefly larvae climb onto utility poles and pupate—from the Latin *pupa*, "doll," which designates the intermediate stage between larva and imago, sometimes called a *nymph*—dangerously exposed to diurnal predators and to sunshine that dries and kills them. We must know that, *in spite of all*, fireflies have formed their beautiful, luminous communities *elsewhere* (by association, I'm reminded of a few images from the end of *Fahrenheit 451*, when the main character escapes the city limits and finds himself in the community of book lovers).

It goes without saying that, under these conditions, fireflies form an anachronistic [*achronique*], atopian community (Figure 1). They are, however, on the agenda, perhaps even at the center of our modern scientific discussions. The Nobel Prize in Chemistry was recently awarded to Osamu Shimomura: a *hibakusha* who survived radiation from the American bomb dropped on Nagasaki on August 9, 1945, when he was seventeen years old, and who would dedicate his entire life as a researcher to phenomena of bioluminescence observable in certain jellyfish, his specialization, but also in our beloved fireflies.[9] Beginning in 1887, the physiologist Raphael Dubois isolated in Lampyridae an enzyme that he wanted to call *luciferase*, which acts on a chemical substrate, *luciferin*, in the bioluminescent phenomenon of fireflies (clearly we never stop returning to the devil and to hell, whose fire—the evil light—is never very far away).

It would be criminal and stupid to place fireflies under a spotlight, expecting to observe them better. Just as it's useless to study them having killed them beforehand, pinning them to the

Figure 1. Renata Siqueira Bueno, *Lucioles,* 2008. Serra de Canastra, Brazil.

entomologist's table and staring at them as if they were very old things, trapped in amber for millions of years.[10] To understand fireflies, we must see them in the present of their survival: we must see them alive and dancing in the heart of the night, even if that night may be swept by fierce spotlights. And even if only for a short time. And even if there isn't much to see: it takes around five thousand fireflies to produce light equivalent to that of a single candle. Just as there is a minor literature—as Gilles Deleuze and Félix Guattari showed, related to Franz Kafka—this would be a *minor light,* possessing the same philosophical characteristics: "a high coefficient of deterritorialization"; "everything in them is political"; "everything takes on a collective value," such that everything speaks of the people and of the "revolutionary conditions" that are immanent in their very marginalization.[11]

In 1975, believing that he had observed the irremediable disappearance of fireflies, Pasolini would do nothing but immobilize himself in a sort of grief, a sort of political despair. As if, all at once, he gave up lifting his gaze toward those unlikely parts of our societies that he had once described so well; as if he could no longer get moving himself, as he had done so well when making *Accattone* in the impoverished zones of the Roman suburbs, with Sergio Citti—brother of Franco, who played Accattone—as a "living dictionary" of the Romanesco dialect. "I spent the most beautiful days of my life this way," Pasolini wrote about these incursions into a region of humanity that was still invisible—marginal, minor—to most of his contemporaries.[12] But in 1975, Pasolini postulated the unity without recourse of a society enslaved in its totality, and without any fear of contradicting himself: "It's an apocalyptic vision, certainly. But if, along with that apocalyptic vision and the anxiety it provokes, there weren't also some bit of optimism in me, in other words the idea that it's possible to struggle against all that, I would very simply not be here, among you, to speak."[13]

It's not useful to fall back on biography to understand the fundamental link that, for Pasolini, ties the image of fireflies—in 1941 as in 1975—to something that one could call a political history of sexuality or, better yet, a sexualized history of politics. In 1974, for example, Jean-François Lyotard published his *Libidinal Economy,*[14] while Michel Foucault was starting his major research on *The History of Sexuality* in the West.[15] For his part, Pasolini had long understood, for example, in his 1965 documentary *Love Meetings,* that accepted or marginal forms of sexuality imply or suppose a certain political position that never exists—as in love—without a certain *dialectic of desire.* The sad thing is that, in 1975, Pasolini's sex life was under the heat of the spotlights, that his *Trilogy of Life* had been released, as in Alain Brossat's analysis, into the marketplace of cultural tolerance; as a result, his despair was inextricably connected to sexual desire and the desire for political emancipation.

But to this "illuminated" despair, we must contrast the fact that the fireflies' living dance plays out precisely in the heart of shadows. And that it is nothing other than a *dance of community-forming desire* (the very thing that Pasolini was to stage in the very last shot of *Salò*, the very thing that he was still seeking, no doubt, on that beach in Ostia, just before the appearance of headlights on the car that crushed and mangled him). The male fireflies' phosphorescent organs occupy three segments of the abdomen, in the females, only two. Although some animal species use bioluminescence to attract prey or to defend against predators (for example, to frighten the enemy by emitting an unexpected burst of light), fireflies use biolumi-nescence first and foremost as a sexual display. No, fireflies do not light up in order to light a world they'd like to "see better."[16] A good example of sexual display is given by the *Odontosyllis*, a glowworm in Bermuda: "Coupling takes place during the full moon, fifty-five minutes after sunset. First, the females appear on the surface and swim rapidly, describing circles and emitting a bright glow that looks like a halo.... The males then climb from the bottom of the sea, also emitting light, but in the form of flashes. They go directly to the center of the halo and turn in time with the females for a few seconds, letting out their sperm with a luminous exudate. The light then disappears suddenly."[17]

In the southern regions of Europe where the species called *Luciola italica,* or the Italian firefly, predominates, things hap-pen differently, and differently on the American continent as well, as Claude Gudin describes in his *Histoire naturelle de la séduction*: "We are all familiar with these small, yellow luminous signals that glowworms emit on our summer nights. These are the larvae of a small beetle of the Lampyridae family. It is unknown why the larvae are luminescent, but we know that the female, who retains a larval appearance even in maturity, attracts the flying males with her two small lanterns in the corner of a bush. As to their American cousins, fireflies of the *Photinus* genus, the males and females communicate to each other using numerous flashes. So the fireflies' mating display in both the Old and the New World, adapted to night, occurs by luminescence, with or without colors that are normally visible by day. This doesn't happen entirely without malice. Female *Photuris* fireflies respond to the flashes of males in flight, a luminous conversation follows, and the two lovers couple. But after this, the female adopts the flash sequence of another *Photinus* firefly, lures the males that land nearby, and devours them. There, it is clear that Lucifer meddles."[18]

With this new mention of the devil, Lucifer, "carrier of light"—or of evil—the primary issue is simply the cruel game of *attraction* inherent to the entire animal kingdom: the gift of life and the gift of death each in its turn, the call to reproduce and the call to mutual destruction. At the center of all these phenomena, bioluminescence illustrates a major principle, introduced into ethology by Adolf Portmann: there is no living community without a phenomenology of *presentation* in which each individual confronts—attracts or repulses, desires or devours, seeks or avoids—the other.[19] Fireflies present themselves to others of their kind by a sort of *mimicking act* that has the extraordinary feature of being nothing but an intermittent dash of light, a signal, a gesture in a sense.[20] Today we know that on the most fundamental level, whether in the visible spectrum or in the ultraviolet, all living beings emit a photon flux.[21]

But this was Pasolini's political despair in 1975: like fireflies, the human creatures of our contemporary societies had been vanquished, annihilated, pinned down, or dried out under the artificial glare of spotlights, under the panoptical eyes of surveillance cameras, under the deadening agitation of television screens. In Pasolini's eyes, "human beings no longer exist" in societies of control—like those of which Michel Foucault and Gilles Deleuze sketched out the general functioning—and there is no more living community. There are no more signals to exchange, only signs to brandish. There is nothing left to desire. Thus nothing left to see, or to hope for. The flashes, the glimmers—as one says, a "glimmer of hope"—have disappeared along with innocence, condemned to death. But for us, reading Pasolini today with emotion, admiration, and agreement, a question arises here: why was he so despairingly mistaken, and why did he then radicalize his own despair? Why did his own light, his own brilliance as a political writer, come so suddenly to be consumed, to be extinguished, dried out, annihilated of its own accord?

For it wasn't the fireflies that had been destroyed; rather, it was something central in Pasolini's desire to see—in his desire in general, and thus in his political hope. The external reasons for this decline are generally understood: the constant attacks on him, the failure—linked to the triumph—of *The Trilogy of Life*, and so many things that we can easily find in the filmmaker's biography. But what were the intrinsic reasons, linked to the very form of his language? What movement within his thought carried Pasolini toward this despair without recourse, or rather with no other recourse than to assert himself [*s'affirmer*] one last time, ardently, like a moth in the last seconds of its tragic and luminous consummation? Of course I realize that, in posing this question, it is not so much Pasolini *for his own sake* that I'm striving to understand better but rather a certain discourse— poetic or philosophical, artistic or polemic, philosophical or historical—held today in his wake, a discourse that attempts to make meaning *for us,* for our contemporary situation.

For the consequences of this modest case in point could very well be considerable, beyond even the extreme, hyperbolic significance that Pasolini would confer to them. In effect, it means nothing more nor less than rethinking our own "principle of hope," through the manner in which the Past meets the Present to form a glimmer, a flash, a constellation in which some form for our very Future suddenly breaks free.[22] Although they skim just above the ground, moving so slowly, emitting such a weak light, don't the fireflies draw, strictly speaking, just such a constellation? To assert this about the minor example of fireflies is to assert also that in our *way of imagining* lies a fundamental condition of *our way of doing politics*. Imagination is political; this is what we need to understand. Inversely, as Hannah Arendt showed starting from very general premises pulled from the philosophy of Kant, politics does not work, from one moment to another, without the ability to imagine.[23] And it's no surprise that, in a crucial moment of the long-running political reflection that he has undertaken, Jacques Rancière must concentrate on questions of the image, the imagination, and the "distribution of the sensible."[24]

If imagination—this work that produces images for thought—enlightens us through the way that, there, the Past meets our Now, to free the rich constellations of the Future, then we can understand just how decisive is that encounter of times, that collision between an active present and a reminiscent past. It was Walter Benjamin, no doubt, who posed the problem of historical time in general.[25] But first it was Aby Warburg who showed not only the constitutive role of *survivals* in the dynamic of the Western imagination but also the *political* functions that their organizations of memory are revealed as carrying out. This is especially evident in one of the great art historian's last articles, on the usage of pagan divination in the political writings and images of the Lutheran reform, or yet again in questions of political theology that appear in the very last plates of his *Mnemosyne Atlas* of images.[26]

Close as Pasolini was historically and intellectually to Ernesto de Martino, the great Italian anthropologist of survivals—who worked on the long tradition of ritual lament and on the history of the apocalyptic imagination[27]—he knew, poetically and visually, what *survival* meant. He understood the indestructible character, transmitted here, invisible but latent there, resurging elsewhere, of images in perpetual metamorphosis. This is what appears in his films, up to and including the most "contemporary"—I'm thinking, for example, of Laura Betti's gestures in *Theorem*—and, it goes without saying, in all his mythological, religious, or "medieval" films. It's what determines the intentional conjunction of the archaic and the contemporary in his work, as he directed Orson Welles to say in *La Ricotta*: "More modern than any modern . . . I am a force from the Past."[28] Let's not forget that in the film, this phrase is pronounced by an artist, himself weighted with experience and his love of history. But this artist is sitting across from a journalist, who is incapable of anything other than breaking down all the *depth of the contemporary* into the *platitudes of the day,* necessary to the society of the spectacle.

In the instance of *La Ricotta,* then, Pasolini manages—rather superbly—to reclaim a dialectical position: his narrative is itself constructed as the collision between the Past (filmed in color) and the Now (filmed in black and white). So that, cruel as the end of poor Stracchi may seem, the entire film appears to be taking a position—effective, disturbing, inventive, joyous—on the relationship between history (art history in particular) and the present (of Italian society). But it seems that, in 1975, having renounced his last three films and at work in the infernal bolgia of *Salò*, Pasolini despaired of all impertinence, of all dialectical joy. It is thus the *disappearance of survivals*—or the disappearance of the anthropological conditions of resistance to Italian neofascism's centralized power—that is at issue in the small case study that the fireflies' disappearance represents.

The objection that one could address to Pasolini regarding the "disappearance of fireflies" would be formulated, then, in these terms: how can one proclaim the death of survivals? Isn't it just as futile as decreeing the deaths of our obsessions, of our memories in general? Isn't it giving in to the tired inference, from a phrase like *Desire isn't what it used to be* to a phrase like *There is no more desire?* What the filmmaker had seen so masterfully in the present of the 1950s and 1960s—the survivals at work and the resistance efforts of the subproletariat in *Stories from the City of God,* in *Accattone,* or in *Mamma Roma*—was lost from his view in the present of the 1970s. From then on, he could no longer see where or how the Past impacted the Now to produce the small flashes and constellations of fireflies. He despaired of his time, nothing more (and all his supposedly "reactionary" positions of this period can be understood through such a lens, whether they concerned student revolts, long hair on young men, sexual liberation, or abortion). Despairing, Pasolini could ultimately only lose the dialectical game of gaze and imagination. What had disappeared in him was the ability to see—in the night as under the fierce glare of spotlights—that which had not completely disappeared and, above all, that which *appears in spite of all* as reminiscent newness, as "innocent" newness, in the present of this detestable history from which he could no longer escape, even on the inside.

3

Apocalypses?

A lovely dialectical vision on one side: the ability to recognize a resistance in the smallest firefly, a light for all thought. On the other, nondialectical despair: the inability to see new fireflies once the first ones—the "fireflies of youth"—are lost from sight. It's the same kind of problematic configuration that I seem to recognize in recent texts of Giorgio Agamben, one of the most important and most troubling philosophers of our time. What more could we ask of a thinker than to *trouble his time* by having his own troublesome relationship with history, as to the present? It's no surprise that Giorgio Agamben is a great reader of Walter Benjamin. It's no surprise that he is, after Edgar Wind, one of the very rare philosophers to take a full theoretical account of the anthropology of survivals that Aby Warburg elaborated.[1] *Stanzas* is a superbly Benjaminian book, in the sense that it is the exact sort of work that Benjamin began in his *Arcades Project* and planned to develop as a sort of "documentary work" *(Dokumentarwerk),* with its object being imagination itself.[2] Not by chance, Agamben composed this book, in part, between the shelves—exalted shelves, at once inexhaustible mines of knowledge and imaginative machines—of the Warburg Library in London.

As some of his most recent texts demonstrate so luminously, Giorgio Agamben is not a philosopher of dogmas but one of *paradigms*: for him, the most humble objects, the most varied images, become—alongside the long-canonical philosophical texts that he discusses and comments on without pause—occasion for an "epistemology of the example" and a veritable "philosophical archaeology," which, again in a very Benjaminian way, "moves backward through the course of history, just as the imagination" itself goes back to the origins of things outside of the great conceptual theologies.[3] Bringing *sources* to light appears here as the necessary condition—and the patient work—of a thought that does not immediately seek to take a side but rather to *interrogate the contemporary* in the light of its occult philology, its hidden traditions, its nonthoughts, its survivals.

Much differently, then, from philosophers who offer themselves as dogmaticians for eternity or as instant opinion makers for the present moment—regarding the latest technological gadget, the latest presidential election—Agamben envisions the contemporary within the considerable and complex density of its entangled temporalities. Thus the montage aspect, also Warburgian and Benjaminian, that his texts often have. For Agamben, there is no contemporary other than that which appears "through a disjunction and an anachronism" in relation to everything we perceive as our "reality."[4] To be contemporary, in this sense, would mean obscuring the spectacle of the present century so as to perceive, in that very obscurity, the "light that strives to reach us but cannot."[5] Returning to the paradigm that concerns us here, it would mean giving oneself the means to *see fireflies appear* in the fierce, overexposed, overbright space of our current history. This task, Agamben adds, demands at once courage—political virtue—and poetry, the art of fracturing language, of breaking down appearances, of disassembling the unity of time.[6]

These are the same two virtues that Pasolini deploys in each of his texts, in each of his images. Between Pasolini and

Agamben, of course, the historical and philosophical references present considerable differences. But the general *gestus* of their respective thoughts hints of an undeniable kinship, up to and including their provocative effects and the virulent attacks often set off by the positions they take. Both Pasolini and Agamben argue that "there is a secret affinity between the archaic and the modern."[7] Both make their work into a stubborn connection between the present—violently criticized—and other times,[8] which is a way of recognizing the necessity of *temporal montages* for all substantial reflection on the contemporary. Like Pasolini, Agamben is a great *profaner* of things that the general consensus deems "sacred." And like the filmmaker when he spoke of the "sacral," the philosopher attempts to rethink the anthropological paradigm contained in the very long history of the word *sacer.*

To my knowledge, Agamben has never made any specific study of Pasolini's poetry or films. But he himself played a part in Pasolini's cinema, very early on, when he incarnated one of Christ's twelve apostles in *The Gospel According to Saint Matthew,* in 1964. It's especially striking to find a set of reflections in the philosopher's work that matches the dramaturgical and anthropological preoccupations of the poet-filmmaker: the admiration for slang and the "antique" force of popular movements, notably in Neapolitan culture[9]—a recurring reflection on the idea of movement [*geste*] and its deep temporality.[10] And finally, an ethical attention regarding "whatever" human face, attention that, deep down, perhaps owes less to the thought of Emmanuel Levinas than to Pasolini's loving practice of the close-up.[11] The languages of the people, their gestures, their faces: all things that *history* cannot account for, with its simple terms of evolution or obsolescence. All things that, by contrast, define zones or networks of *survivals,* even in the space of their extraterritoriality, their marginalization, their resistance, their calling to revolt.

And yet, Agamben's first book explicitly related to the question of *history* is inscribed, in its subtitle, with the word *destruction*.[12] This word sounds a merciless diagnosis of the present times, a diagnosis announced abruptly in the very first lines of the work: "The question of experience can be approached nowadays only with an acknowledgment that it is no longer accessible to us. For just as modern man has been deprived of his biography, his experience has likewise been expropriated. Indeed, his incapacity to have and communicate experiences is perhaps one of the few self-certainties to which he can lay claim."[13] Written only a few months after Pasolini's essay on the disappearance of fireflies, these words proceed from the same basic logic. First, they both make reference to a situation of *manifest apocalypse,* an apocalypse that is concrete, undeniable, explosive, meaning a situation of military conflict. Agamben brings up not historical fascism but the First World War, the mental landscape that Walter Benjamin had explored in "Experience and Poverty" in 1933, then in "The Storyteller" in 1936, a text to which Agamben refers explicitly, of which the central passage is as follows:

> It is as if a capability that seemed inalienable to us, the securest among our possessions, has been taken from us: the ability to share experiences.
>
> One reason for this phenomenon is obvious: experience has fallen in value. And it looks as if it may fall into bottomlessness. Every glance at a newspaper shows that it has reached a new low—that our image not only of the external world but also of the moral world has undergone changes overnight, changes which were previously thought impossible. Beginning with the First World War, a process became apparent which continues to this day. Wasn't it noticeable at the end of the war that men who returned from the battlefield had grown silent—not richer, but poorer in communicable experience? What poured out in the flood of war books ten years later was anything but experience that can be shared orally.

And there was nothing remarkable about that. For never has experience been more thoroughly belied than strategic experience was belied by tactical warfare, economic experience by inflation, bodily experience by mechanical warfare, moral experience by those in power. A generation that had gone to school on horse-drawn streetcars now stood under the open sky in a countryside in which nothing remained unchanged but the clouds, and beneath those clouds, in a force field of destructive torrents and explosions, the tiny, fragile human body.[14]

Next—and still following the same logic as Pasolini's 1975 essay—Agamben evokes the present time as a situation of *latent apocalypse,* where it seems as if there is no more conflict, yet destruction nevertheless ravages every body and every spirit, even in the most innocent mass phenomena—tourism, for example:

Today, however, we know that the destruction of experience no longer necessitates a catastrophe, and that humdrum daily life in any city will suffice. For modern man's average day contains virtually nothing that can still be translated into experience. Neither reading a newspaper, with its abundance of news that is irretrievably remote from his life, nor sitting for minutes on end at the wheel of his car in a traffic jam. Neither the journey through the netherworld of the subway, nor the demonstration that suddenly blocks the street. Neither the cloud of tear gas slowly dispersing through the buildings of the city centre, nor the rapid blasts of gunfire from who knows where, nor queuing up at a business counter, nor visiting the Land of Cockayne at the supermarket, nor those eternal moments of dumb promiscuity among strangers in lifts and buses. Modern man makes his way home in the evening wearied by a jumble of events, but however entertaining or tedious, unusual or commonplace, harrowing or pleasurable they are, none of them will have become experience.

It is this non-translatability into experience that now makes everyday existence intolerable—as never before. From this

> point of view a visit to a museum or a place of touristic pil-
> grimage is particularly instructive. Standing face to face with
> one of the great wonders of the world (let us say the *patio de
> los leones* in the Alhambra), the overwhelming majority of
> people have no wish to experience it, preferring instead that
> the camera should. Of course the point is not to deplore this
> state of affairs, but to take note of it.[15]

This description of the present time—constructed on the basis
of a total war situation—constitutes a veritable philosophical
matrix: from this description will follow, in the course of the
text, a whole series of reflections in which the word *crisis,* for
example, transforms inescapably into a radical *lack,* in which
all transformation will be considered as destruction, just as one
sees in this despairing judgment on the history of modern poetry
after Baudelaire, the poet of a "crisis of experience": "modern poetry from Baudelaire onwards is seen to be founded not on new
experience, but on an unprecedented lack of experience"[16]—an
untenable proposition, it seems to me, considering the smallest
texts by Rilke, Michaux, René Char, Bertolt Brecht, Paul Celan.
Or Pasolini himself, by the way. We are left with the impres-
sion, in fact, that Agamben would take up exactly where the
filmmaker left off in 1975: at the exact point where the *eulogy
for childhood*—inherent in his 1941 letter, and up through the
films in *The Trilogy of Life*—transforms into *mourning for all
childhood.* From here comes the definition, negative and then
transcendental, of childhood or infancy [*enfance*] in Agamben.
"*The ineffable is, in reality, infancy.* . . . It is infancy, it is the transcendental experience of the difference between language and
speech":[17] an *originary* experience, certainly, but one that has
been destroyed, *extinguished* like a firefly, in our poor present day.

How does Agamben proceed here? First, he asserts a radical
destruction—next, he constructs a transcendence. Such would
be the philosophical matrix, the movement that structures this

anxiety and this power of thought. Most of the paradigms that the philosopher elaborates over the long course of his work seem to be marked, in fact, by something that, *unhappily,* cuts implicitly across the extraordinary acuity of his gaze: like the swing of a pendulum between the extremes of *destruction* and a sort of *redemption* through transcendence. In his essay on the *Muselmann* of the Nazi concentration camps, for example, Agamben begins with the "untestifiable" and the "impossibility of vision" to evoke, at the other end of his course, a transcendental—in a sense sublime, as in Lyotard—condition of the "essential witness" and the "absolute image."[18] In *Means without End*—a book dedicated, significantly, to Guy Debord—the "absolute, integral" dimension of the gesture and its "mystical" value in Wittgenstein's sense are affirmed only on the basis of a destruction, of mourning at departure: "By the end of the nineteenth century, the Western bourgeoisie had definitely lost its gestures."[19] As if everything owed its philosophical dignity only to its having first disappeared, destroyed by some neofascism or some society of the spectacle, from our common world.

As Pasolini himself admitted, this is indeed an "apocalyptic vision." Or rather *an apocalyptic way of "seeing the time" at work,* and seeing the present time in particular. When Pasolini announces that "human beings no longer exist," or when Giorgio Agamben, for his part, claims that the contemporary person's "experience has been expropriated," we find ourselves, again and again, placed under the blinding light of an apocalyptic space and time. Apocalypse: this is a major theme of the Judeo-Christian religious tradition. It would be the survival that absorbs all others in its devouring brilliance: the great "sacral" survival—the end times, the time of the Last Judgment—when all others will have been put to death. The great survival proclaimed to put to death all the others, all those "small" survivals that we experience here and there in our wandering, like so many glimmers in the *selva oscura,* where hope and memory send each other their mutual signals.

In contrast to this humble experience, apocalyptic visions offer us the grandiose landscape of a radical *destruction* to bring on the *revelation* of a higher, no less radical truth. Can't we recognize here the old metaphysical refrain, Aristotle's statement of "quiddity" in the form of *to ti èn einaï* (what the thing was)? Wouldn't the *being* then be stated in the *past?* Would it be revealed only once it has *passed away?* We can understand here that, for the metaphysician, the death of his object is necessary to pronounce in any definitive way on its *final truth.*[20] From destroyed realities, then, to final truths: such is the philosophers' "apocalyptic tone" when, rather than small "glimmers of truth"—which are inevitably provisory, empirical, intermittent, fragile, disparate, passing, like fireflies—they choose a great "light of truth" that reveals, instead, a transcendent *light on light,* or on lights, each in its own shadowy corner, bound to disappear, to flee elsewhere.

Taking Kant's short essay titled "On a Newly Arisen Superior Tone in Philosophy"[21] as a basis, Jacques Derrida attempted a critique of this "apocalyptic tone" adopted—today as in the past—by a number of "radical" thinkers, of which he himself was one. "Every apocalyptic eschatology," he wrote, "is promised in the name of light, of visionary and vision, of a light of light, of a light brighter than all the lights it makes possible. . . . There would be no truth of the apocalypse that was not the truth of the truth, . . . truth of the revelation rather than revealed truth."[22] Derrida then affirms that "this demystification [of the apocalyptic tone] must be led as far as possible, and the task is not modest. It is interminable, because no one can exhaust the overdeterminations and the indeterminations of the apocalyptic stratagems. And above all because the ethicopolitical motif or motivation of these strategems is never reducible to some simple."[23] From one angle, then, the Kantian critique of the "mystagogues" of thought must extend to a critique of catastrophic or redemptive figures of all kinds, from the master of sectarian thought up to the totalitarian *Führer*.[24] But from another angle, Derrida tries to find a voice in the apocalyptic phrase, a voice [*voix*] that, like Nietzsche or Maurice Blanchot, would be an *envoy* [*envoi*], finding the *way* [*voie*] in a statement like *Come*.[25] Critique ends up reabsorbed in a discourse of announcement that would be, undecidably, "apocalypse without apocalypse" or truth "without vision, without truth, without revelation."[26]

But this critique—what Agamben is attempting for his own part, it seems to me—is it only possible? To this general hypothesis, to this well-intentioned philosophical project, couldn't one address the same critique that Adorno made to Heidegger, in terms of the *impossible secularization* of a metaphysical thought that maintains the most fundamental structures of a theological world, of which recovery is in no sense *profanation*? It's worth remembering the passage in which Adorno explains his critique of the place of the *unthought of the resurrection* in Heidegger: "I would say that the approach adopted in *Being and Time*...is perhaps nowhere more ideological than when its author tries to understand death on the basis of 'Dasein's possibility of Being-a-Whole,' in which attempt he suppresses the absolute irreconcilability of living experience with death which has become apparent with the definitive decline of positive religions. He seeks, in this way, to rescue structures of the experience of death as structures of *Dasein,* of human existence itself. But these structures, as he describes them, only existed within the world of positive theology, by virtue of the positive hope of the resurrection; and Heidegger fails to see that through the secularization of this structure, which he at least tacitly assumes in his work, not only have these theological contents disintegrated, but without them this experience itself is no longer possible. What I really hold against this form of metaphysics is the surreptitious attempt to appropriate theologically posited possibilities of experience without theology."[27]

This detour doubtless complicates our discussion a bit on the philosophical level. But it illuminates the very difficulty in which Pasolini might have found himself, for example, when he turned back to the Christian *tradition*—that "positive religion," as Adorno calls it—to give political legitimacy to the *survivals* at work in the popular language and gestures of the Italian "*misérables*."[28] It illuminates, as well, certain theoretical difficulties in which Agamben finds himself, when he works with a Heideggerian historicity along with the Benjaminian dialectical image, or St. Paul's messianism along with a reflection on the "Final Solution" that the Nazis planned for the Jewish people.[29] Only religious tradition promises a *salvation* beyond all apocalypse and beyond all *destruction* of human things. Survivals, though, concern only the immanence of historical time: they have no redemptive value. And as to their revelatory value, it is always spotty, in flickers: symptomatic, to be honest. Survivals promise no resurrection (what meaning could one expect from raising a ghost?). They are nothing but glimmers, flashes passing in the shadows, never the advent of a great "light of lights." Because they teach us that destruction—even ongoing destruction—is never absolute, survivals spare us from believing that a "last" revelation or a "final" salvation is necessary for our freedom.

By definition, a "politics of survivals" has no need for—necessarily does without—the end times. To my knowledge, Warburg never made any allusion to this on the level of method: he spoke only from a historical and symptomal perspective, much like Ernesto de Martino after him.[30] There is an ambiguity, then, on the level of method as well as on the political level, in passing, as Agamben often does, from an anthropological reflection on the *power [puissance] of survivals* to a philosophical assumption about the *power [pouvoir] of traditions*. Such is, for example, the Italian philosopher's interpretation of messianic times according to St. Paul: on one hand, it begins with a rather precious reference to the Benjaminian *image* as the "now of its 'legibility'" and "of its 'knowability.'"[31] But on the other hand, this interpretation reappropriates the theological *horizon* of the entire Judeo-Christian tradition to make it into a political paradigm, which becomes forcefully apparent in the philosopher's latest work, *The Kingdom and the Glory.*[32]

And yet *image* is not *horizon*. The image offers us a few nearby glimmers *(lucciole)*, while the horizon promises a great and faraway light *(luce)*. This distinction, concerning the fundamental—but oh-so-problematic—relationship between thoughts on history, political positions, and messianic traditions, may seem precious in separating the recourse to survivals from the return to tradition in thinkers like Franz Rosenzweig and Walter Benjamin, on one side,[33] Carl Schmitt and Ernst Jünger, on the other. As Stéphane Mosès demonstrated in one of his last texts, Benjaminian messianism, building on Rosenzweig, concerns a lacunary *image* of the future and not a great *horizon* of salvation or end times.[34] The famous "small gateway" of messianism opens only a crack, for "a second," Benjamin writes[35]—about the time that a firefly takes to flash, to call to its companions, just before darkness restakes its claim.

The image is characterized by its intermittence, its fragility, its pulse of appearance and disappearance, of reappearances and redisappearances without end. So it's an entirely different thing to think of the messianic moment as image (before which one could not nurse any illusions for long, because the image will disappear *soon*) than to think of it as horizon (which calls to a unilateral faith, oriented, supported by the thought of a permanent beyond, even if *forever* awaiting its future). The image isn't much: a remnant, a crack. An accident of the time that renders it momentarily visible or readable.[36] Whereas the horizon promises us the whole, constantly hidden behind its great fleeing "line." "One of the reasons I'm keeping such a distance from all these horizons," writes Derrida in "Force of Law," "from the Kantian regulative idea or from the messianic advent, for example, or at least from their conventional interpretation—is that they are, precisely, *horizons*. As its Greek name suggests, a horizon is both the opening and the limit that defines an infinite progress or a period of waiting."[37]

The complexity of Agamben's thought insists, perhaps, that the regimes of the image and of the horizon are constantly mixed or surreptitiously adjoined, as if the first—which is an empirical regime of local *approach* and local approximation—had no value but to free up the immense space of the second, the regime of the *faraway,* of the apogee, the absolute. As a reader of Benjamin, Agamben is a philosopher of the image (a bit like Pasolini, when he constructed his films using *fragments* or close-ups); hence the manner of philology through which we discover, often with wonder, the hidden power of the slightest gesture, the slightest letter, the slightest face, the slightest glimmer and flash.[38] But as a reader of Heidegger, Agamben seeks the horizon behind every image (a little like Pasolini when he decided to judge the *whole* and the ends of the civilization in which he lived). And yet that horizon inevitably reshapes the metaphysical cosmos, the philosophical system, the juridical corpus or theological dogma.

In this way, *The Kingdom and the Glory* is presented as a great philological interrogation, focusing on two fundamental aspects: on one hand, the *world of sources,* in which Agamben shows us a fundamental "scission of sovereignty" between "kingdom" and "government."[39] Philological erudition, the gloss and the archaeological method—that of Michel Foucault, but even more so that of Ernst Kantorowicz, for example[40]—seem to occupy the role in Agamben's thought that, in Pasolini's thought, is granted to poetry: they give form to power, to the violence intrinsic to his thought. On the other hand, it is the *world of ends* that opens up to our view and that concerns, from here on, our own contemporary situation. But all of this against the background of a terrible, hopeless or hope-crushing, unacceptable political equivalence between extremes, both drowning in the same horizon, in the same blinding brilliance of power.

4

Peoples

What disappears, in that fierce *light of power,* is nothing other than the slightest image or *glimmer of a counterforce.* This is why Giorgio Agamben cites the Jewish Walter Benjamin in the same breath as the Nazi Carl Schmitt and the communist Pasolini in the same breath as the fascist character in his own film, *Salò:* "Benjamin was in this sense right when he wrote that there is nothing more anarchic than the bourgeois order. Similarly, the remark of one of the Fascist dignitaries in Pasolini's film *Salò* according to which 'the only real anarchy is that of power' is perfectly serious."[1] Benjamin, as we know, used certain concepts from Schmitt's *Political Theology* in his own work, particularly the famous "state of exception," an idea that Agamben himself has expanded in his analysis of our contemporary societies.[2] But for Benjamin, the sole purpose of using Schmitt's concept was to invert the content: to substitute for the *tradition of power*—which is radicalized and totalized in the Nazi politics that Schmitt himself formulated[3]—a *tradition of the oppressed* that, in Benjamin's time, was characterized by the struggle at all costs against fascism: "The tradition of the oppressed teaches us that the 'state of emergency' in which we live is not the exception but the rule. We must attain to a conception of history that accords with this insight. Then we will clearly see that it is our task to bring about a real state of emergency, and this will improve our position in the struggle against fascism."[4]

In his own use of Carl Schmitt, Agamben seems to follow in the footprints of Jacob Taubes, extending Taubes's commentaries on the long history of eschatological thought as well as his shorter lectures on St. Paul.[5] Taubes attempted to clarify his recourse to Schmitt through the expression—borrowed from a Hericlitean vocabulary—of *gegenstrebige Füfung* [*palintropos harmonie*], the "tensed bow." Stigmatized as a Jew and an enemy by the current of thought from which he nonetheless derived his own theoretical energy, Taubes formulated a diagnosis of great clarity on the case of Martin Heidegger, as of Carl Schmitt: "These are people driven by a resentment . . . but who, with the genius of the resentful, reread the sources," and in doing so, they reveal better than anyone the very horizon of all Western thought on power.[6]

But in refusing to "judge" these same thinkers who formalized his exclusion as a radical enemy,[7] Taubes was already sparing himself, it seems to me, from understanding the fissure, the point of bifurcation that decisively separates a concept, rigorously and legitimately formulated—whether that is "sovereignty" or the "state of exception"[8]—from the choices by which one may put that concept into practice. And yet those choices are themselves oriented by a horizon: the whole question is knowing what one wants to do with a concept, whatever it may be, and to what end one wants to put it in operation. One of the rare moments when Taubes clearly marks his choice, that is, his protest, his positioning within the debate that he carries out with Carl Schmitt, is when he writes, "You see what I want from Schmitt—to show him that the division of powers between the terrestrial and the spiritual orders is *absolutely necessary*; if this demarcation is not made, then we are lost. It was this that I wanted to put to him against his totalitarian orientation."[9]

Rather than making claims for *division* as opposed to the

totalization of power, as Taubes does here, Giorgio Agamben's recent contribution to this debate comes down to observing that division even in the most totalizing forms of sovereignty, for example, in the "distinction between Kingdom and Government," a distinction of long standing that Schmitt, Agamben says, "re-elaborates from a new perspective" at the same moment in 1933 when, on Hitler's behalf, Schmitt was reflecting on the relationships between "state," "movement" (meaning the Nazi party), and "people."[10] In his thought on sovereignty, then, the author of *Homo Sacer* positions himself beyond all division as beyond all totalization: the latter would always be divided and the former always totally, radically in effect in this genealogy of Western power.[11]

And this is the paradox of such an *economy*—a central word in all of Agamben's analysis—that allows one to "seriously" accept the witticism from *Salò*'s torturer: "The only real anarchy is that of power."[12] So there would be no distinction to make—whereas Taubes continues to insist on marking its importance—between the "apocalyptic thinkers of the revolution," such as Leon Trotsky, Bertolt Brecht, or Walter Benjamin, and the "apocalyptic thinkers of the counter-revolution," such as Oswald Spengler, Ernst Jünger, Martin Heidegger, or Carl Schmitt himself.[13] What gets lost, in such a horizon of thought, is nothing other than the possibility of making a response or a riposte to the economy of power so described. Agamben knows very well—reading Guy Debord, for example—that there is no *kingdom* and no *glory* without the destructive effects of *oppression* and *shadows*. But he does not bother to speak of these, as if he can no longer see anything but the blinding light of the kingdom and its glory. Where, then, has the "true state of exception" gone, what Benjamin still called for in his theses in 1940, in the framework of his own "struggle against fascism"? Is it possible to make a genealogy of power without considering the countersubject constituted by the "tradition of the oppressed"? Where, then, in such an economy, have all the fireflies gone?

In all of this, the fireflies are undergoing nothing less— metaphorically, I mean—than the fate of all peoples *exposed to disappearing*. In the early 1970s, Pasolini still showed all the same power to see and move: he left Italy for Eritrea, a trip with the purpose of scouting and casting for his film, *Arabian Nights*. There, nothing but fireflies—an incomparable succession of wonders before the luminosity, the beauty of the people he encountered: "I was moved almost to tears by those delicate, slightly irregular features . . . , this violence that was not without grace, that was a part of the life . . . of a population in revolt. . . . I fixed my choice then on Fessazion Gherentiel, the bartender at one of those little bars, a brilliant vision, his smile exploding across his face like a silent light,"[14] *e così via*. But two years later, back in Rome, the fierce spotlights of neofascism would blur all this: Pasolini would *let the people disappear*—"Unfortunately I loved them, those people . . ."—he would abandon them to the Kingdom's law, to the Glory's light. From then on the people were, in his eyes, *fallen [tombé]*. Stylistically speaking, the fireflies article is nothing but an *elegy [tombeau]* to lost peoples.

Once again, Agamben's recent conclusions are not unrelated to such political despair. After two remarkable "archaeological" chapters, dedicated—via Erik Peterson and Carl Schmitt, Andreas Alföldi and Ernst Kantorowicz, Percy Ernst Schramm and Jan Assmann—to the history of ceremonial aspects of power, then to the very notion of "glory" *(Herrlichkeit)*, "de-aestheticized" for the purpose of being better articulated with that of the "kingdom" as such *(Herrschaft)*,[15] Agamben opens a "threshold" that appears as the conclusion of his investigation, albeit a provisory conclusion in the immense archipelago of *Homo Sacer*.[16] An investigation that leads him, finally, "into proximity with the center of the machine that glory envelops with its splendor and songs."[17]

Machine of the kingdom *(Herrschaft)* and spectacle of glory *(Herrlichkeit)*: glory giving the kingdom its very *light,* if not its *voice.* "Perhaps never has an acclamation, in the technical sense of the word, been expressed with so much force and efficacy as was 'Heil Hitler' in Nazi Germany or 'Duce duce' in fascist Italy."[18] And today? "These uproarious and unanimous cries that resounded yesterday in the piazzas of our cities," Agamben responds at first, "appear today to be part of a distant and irrevocable past." Immediately, he wonders, "But is it really so?"[19] We understand then that the question would be better formulated this way: how is it that the victory of Western democracies over the totalitarianism of Nazi Germany and fascist Italy could transform, "secularize," that is, extend a cult phenomenon whose apogee is perfectly staged in Leni Riefenstahl's *Triumph des Willens?*

Yet it is to Schmitt that Agamben turns for a response to this question. He cites *Constitutional Theory,* a 1928 text in which the jurist expresses a conservative critique of the Weimar Republic: "The genuinely assembled people are first a people, and only the genuinely assembled people can do that which pertains distinctly to the activity of this people. They can *acclaim....* When indeed only the people are actually assembled for whatever purpose, to the extent that it does not only appear as an organized interest group, for example, during street demonstrations and public festivals, in theaters, on the running track, or in the stadium, this people engaged in acclamation is present, and it is, at least potentially, a political entity."[20] In the same text where Schmitt evoked a unanimous people assembled in a stadium six years *before* the great protests at Nuremberg—that is, on the *horizon of Nazi totalitarianism*—Giorgio Agamben seeks something like a diagnosis for that which is lost to us today, twenty-four years *after* him, and on *the horizon of democracy* in the West.

But for this, he would need to reduce the "political power" of the people to *acclamation*—Roman, Byzantine, medieval . . . totalitarian—and reduce acclamation to what democracies call *public opinion*: "*Public opinion is the modern type of acclamation.* It is perhaps a diffuse type, and its problem is resolved neither sociologically nor in terms of public law. However, its essence and political significance lie in the fact that it can be understood as an acclamation. There is no democracy and no state without public opinion, as there is no state without acclamation."[21] One wonders, then: what is it that makes public opinion in a democracy an exact equivalent—if there are differences, they are not mentioned—of acclamation in systems of absolute power? Agamben will let Guy Debord answer that question for him: the "society of the spectacle" is to public opinion today what the subjection of the crowd was to totalitarianism yesterday:

> What we wish to focus on is the suggestion that the sphere of glory—of which we have attempted to reconstitute the meaning and archeology—does not disappear in modern democracies, but simply shifts to another area, that of public opinion. If this is true, the problem of the political function of the media in contemporary society that is so widely debated today acquires a new meaning and a new urgency.
>
> In 1967, Guy Debord—in what appears to us as a truism today—diagnosed the planetary transformation of capitalist politics and economy as an "immense accumulation of *spectacles*" in which the commodity and capital itself assume the mediatic form of the image. If we link Debord's analysis with Schmitt's thesis according to which public opinion is the modern form of acclamation, the entire problem of the contemporary spectacle of media domination over all areas of social life assumes a new guise. What is in question is nothing

> less than a new and unheard of concentration, multiplication, and dissemination of the function of glory as the center of the political system. What was confined to the spheres of liturgy and ceremonials has become concentrated in the media and, at the same time, through them it spreads and penetrates at each moment into every area of society, both public and private.... [Thus] the holistic state, founded on the immediate presence of the acclaiming people, and the neutralized state that resolves itself in the communicative forms without subject, are opposed only in appearance. They are nothing but two sides of the same glorious apparatus in its two forms: the immediate and subjective glory of the acclaiming people and the mediatic and objective glory of social communication.[22]

Images—what Agamben reduces here to the "mediatic form of the image"—thus assume, in the contemporary world, the function of a "glory," tied to the machine of the "kingdom": *luminous images* helping, by their very power, to make us into *subservient peoples,* hypnotized by the images' flow. This diagnosis is not wrong, of course. It corresponds to the stifled, anguished sensations that grip us before the calculated proliferation of images, used at once as tools of marketing and as vehicles of propaganda. But in Agamben's book, this diagnosis appears as a *final truth*: the conclusion of his book as much as the apocalyptic horizon under which it falls. So that in the end he de-dialecticizes, he deconflictualizes, he impoverishes both the concept of *images* and that of *peoples.* Here the image is no longer an alternative to the horizon, *la lucciola* an alternative to *la luce.* No longer does it seem to be anything but a pure function of power, incapable of the slightest counterforce, the slightest insurrection, the slightest counterglory. Which indicates something much greater than a simple question of aesthetics, let's remember: the *manifestation of politics* as such, which involves the entire "exhibition value" of peoples in confrontation with the "kingdom" and the "glory," depends on the status of the image—on the use value accorded to it.

If Agamben's discussion ends by establishing a sort of disillusioned equivalence between democracy and dictatorship on the level of an anthropology of "glory," it's because *images* and *peoples* were reduced at the outset, the first to pure processes of subservience, the second to purely subservient bodies. In 1975, Pasolini would certainly have declared his discouragement with the Italian people, but in 1967, the humble masses watching a puppet show in *Che cosa sono le nuvole?* did not hesitate to protest, to rise up out of their seats, to invade the stage—in short, to emancipate themselves through a concrete rupture with the rules that the performance imposed. Allowing Carl Schmitt to speak for him on one hand, and Guy Debord on the other, Agamben sees no alternative to the frightful "glory" of the spectacle. Above all, what he sees in the people is nothing other than what Schmitt and Debord say about them: that is, something that can be defined only *negatively,* by exclusion.

"As should be evident today, people-nation and people-communication, despite the differences in behavior and figure, are the two faces of the *doxa* that, as such, ceaselessly interweave and separate themselves in contemporary society."[23] In such a notion of peoples, all differences are reducible to the same status, the same fate: *doxa,* opinion, belief. That which succumbs to the deceptions of sensible appearances, which thinks poorly and produces false knowledge—in short, everything that philosophical idealism traditionally opposes to the *epistēmē,* to true knowledge, intelligible science, holding correct ideas. This definition comes, perhaps, from very far away, that is, from Plato. But in the economy of Agamben's book, that definition concludes with Schmitt, who, for his part, gathers an entire conservative tradition of the fear of crowds[24] and amplifies it, extends it into a constitutional will to *take* them, to contain them, to render them subservient.

This is what appears in Schmitt's thought, in 1928, in the context of the very pages that Agamben has extracted from *Constitutional Theory*: here the concept of people is first reduced to *unification* of an essence (no multiplicities, no singularities in the people here); second, it is reduced to expressing itself as a simple *negativity*. "According to their nature, the people are *not* a magistrate, and even in a democracy they are never the responsible officials.... The concept of the people is defined in negative terms, in particular by the contrast with the system of administrators and magistrates organized by position. Beyond this negation of the official realm, in other areas it is also characteristic of the concept of the people that it can be defined negatively. It would not only generally involve something sociologically essential, if one defined the people negatively in such a manner (for example, the audience in a theater as part of those present who do *not* perform), but this distinctive negativity also does not permit itself to be mistaken for the scholarly treatment of political theories. In a special meaning of the word, the people are everyone who is *not* honored and distinguished, everyone *not* privileged, everyone prominent *not* because of property, social position, or education."[25]

Finally, we should note that this negative definition is found at the beginning of the chapter in *Constitutional Theory* dedicated to the "boundaries of democracy."[26] And that Schmitt's 1933 text, *State, Movement, People*—which went through three successive editions by 1935—would very logically consecrate the "unity of the people" under the kingdom of the State, under the control of the single party and in the horizon that his final sentence clearly indicates: "All the questions and answers flow into the exigency of an ethnic identity without which a total leader-State could not stand its ground a single day."[27]

In adopting Schmitt's diagnoses, obviously Agamben does
not adopt Schmitt's "therapeutic" goals. But an answer is always
inscribed in the very form of any posed question: it insists, so to
speak. Because Agamben poses the question in these unilateral
terms—these terms that do not admit the least counterform or
"counterquestion"—he closes his inquiry on the dark, steel gray
color of an *unhappy consciousness,* condemned to its own horizon,
to its own closure. Hegel wrote of the unhappy consciousness
and of internal "dividedness" that "consciousness of life, of its
existence and activity, is only an agonizing over this existence
and activity, for therein it is conscious that its essence is only
its opposite, is conscious of its own nothingness."[28] As for
myself, I am unable to imagine a political thought that allows
its enemy to define and control its most fundamental concepts.
From this perspective, we could—and without prejudging the
results in these two examples—compare the *cruel horizon* that
Agamben imagines to the *joyous horizon* that Antonio Negri and
Michael Hardt imagine elsewhere when, to the "empire" of the
contemporary kingdom and glory, they oppose the "multitude"
as a new "possibility of democracy."[29]

Just as Pasolini's opinions, as extreme as they were paradoxical, provoked reactions as scandalized as they were unilateral,
Agamben has found himself criticized with a violence that
often obscures any deeper reading of his work. For example—
and this is only in the French domain—Philippe Mesnard and
Claudine Kahan have excoriated the analysis of the *Muselmann*
that Agamben develops in *Remnants of Auschwitz,* while Éric
Marty attacks the idea of "exception" elaborated in *State of
Exception.*[30] To these unilateral critiques, Agamben responded
very recently that he was being judged on the level of "historical
phenomena"—Auschwitz here, Guantánamo Bay there—when
his analysis had an *archaeological* character and dealt only with

paradigms "whose role was to constitute and make intelligible a broader historical-problematic context."[31]

Agamben articulates philosophically his illumination of paradigms and his archaeological "digging" in history just as, before him, Pasolini articulated poetically his *images* of the present with an energy that he drew from *survivals,* in the sensual archaeology of gestures, songs, dialects, the ruined architecture of Matera, or the neighborhoods of Rome. These two thinkers always show a great impatience for the present, but always linked to an infinite patience for the past. For this, we need them, because they've looked at their contemporary world with a violence always supported by immense research in the thickness of time. In this, too, they shock: because they bring up what is unthought, because they often set before us the return of history's repressed. Of course it's rather unpleasant, when shouting "Forza Italia" in a soccer stadium—even if not necessarily shouting in explicit support of Silvio Berlusconi—to read Agamben's reminders about medieval acclamations and their future in the fascists' "Duce duce."

Agamben and Pasolini interest us most of all, then, on the level of what I have here named *a politics of survivals,* which goes along with any *politics of images* and with political exhibition in general. It is useless to try to refute them simply on a historical level (by arguing, for example, that enthusiasm for soccer has nothing to do with politics, which may be true, or that the detention camp at Guantánamo Bay has nothing to do with Auschwitz, which is true). To me it seems necessary, rather, to debate, to discuss Agamben's constructions on the level where he situates them. And because Walter Benjamin's thought gives these constructions their very condition of possibility, it may be useful to return briefly to the use value of Benjaminian hypotheses, as much on the level of the "archaeological" method as on the level of the illumination of "paradigms."

"Philosophical archaeology," as Agamben has claimed, has its own archaeology, or at the very least its own tradition, marked by the names Kant, Nietzsche, Overbeck, Hermann Usener, Heidegger, Dumézil, Michel Foucault . . . and, of course, Walter Benjamin.[32] Benjamin's contribution is his celebrated essay on the "Angel of History" that "advances toward the future with a gaze fixed on the past."[33] But a more fundamental passage for these questions, while waiting for other texts, more explicit on the idea of archaeological digging,[34] can be found in the "Epistemo-Critical Prologue" of *The Origin of German Tragic Drama,* in which Benjamin constructs the idea of what would be a true "philosophical history, the science of the origin."[35] This, he writes, is "discovered by the examination of actual findings"—which may justify Agamben's defense against his detractors—"but it is related to their history and subsequent development."[36] A way that Benjamin gives a new twist to the *dialectic* as "witness to the origin," in that it "is the form which, in the remotest extremes and the apparent excesses of the process of development, reveals the configuration of the idea—the sum total of all possible meaningful juxtapositions of such opposites."[37] This is also why "that which is original is never revealed in the naked and manifest existence of the factual; its rhythm [*seine Rhythmik*] is apparent only to a dual insight. On the one hand it needs to be recognized as a process of restoration and re-establishment, but, on the other hand, and precisely because of this, as something imperfect and incomplete."[38]

Concretely, this means that a philosophical archaeology, by its very "rhythm," must describe the times and the countertimes, the blows and counterblows, subjects and countersubjects. This means that there is a fundamental lack in a book like *The Kingdom and the Glory* of description of everything that does not belong to the kingdom (meaning the "tradition of the oppressed" and the archaeology of counterforces) or to the glory (meaning the tradition of hidden resistance and the archaeology of "fireflies"). The archaeology of *acclamations,* from Ernst Kantorowicz and Carl Schmitt, lacks an archaeology of *protests,* that is, of *revolutions,* in which peoples have done much more than say *yes* or *no,* by the way, for the eventual *no* of acclamations is subject to the same conditions of ceremony set by the power's authority. It's then that peoples are constituted as political subjects in their own right, so that they may change the rules, and the kingdom, and the glory. Benjamin emphasizes all of this in *Paris, Capital of the Nineteenth Century* or in his "On the Concept of History," when he brings up the French Revolution, the 1848 Revolution, and the Spartacist uprising, or perhaps when he describes the moment of the July Revolution when, "on the first evening of fighting, it so happened that the dials of the clocktowers were being fired at simultaneously and independently from several locations in Paris."[39]

Logically, a *philosophy of paradigms* would take on the work of describing this way to change the rules that, despite its radical newness, finds its source and its recourse in something like a hidden tradition. "The paradigm," Agamben writes, "is a singular case that is isolated from its context only insofar as, by exhibiting its own singularity, it makes intelligible a new ensemble, whose homogeneity it itself constitutes.... That is to say, while induction proceeds from the particular to the universal and deduction from the universal to the particular, the paradigm is defined by a third and paradoxical kind of movement, which goes from the particular to the particular.... [A] paradigm entails a movement that goes from singularity to singularity and, without ever leaving singularity, transforms every singular case into an exemplar of a general rule that can never be stated a priori."[40] And Agamben specifies, regarding this paradoxical and indefinable rule, that "what is essential here is the suspension of reference and normal use."[41]

And yet, what the acclamation paradigm proposes, according to the analysis in *The Kingdom and the Glory*—or rather the conclusions that Agamben draws there, from the combination of Schmitt and Debord—ignores exactly this capacity of suspension, transformation, bifurcation. Schmitt proceeds, rather, by induction, inferring from one particular situation (acclaiming) the universal definition of the people (who know only how to do exactly that, to acclaim). As for Debord, he proceeds more often by deduction, inferring from a universal situation (the society of the spectacle) the totality of individual behaviors, in which every move the people make ends up assimilating to the *doxa,* a powerless variation on acclamation. In short, the paradigm has lost its power: its power as symptom, as exception, as protest in action. It is transmitted, without actually transforming. It can only return, by displacements or secularizations, to the traditional relations of the kingdom and the glory. The irony of the story is that it is a philosopher no doubt very different from Agamben—even hostile to Agamben's work—who provides an exemplary case, a paradigm in which the *voice of the people* may demand its singularity beyond all the ceremony of acclamation: I'm thinking here of that *Cri du peuple* that Jacques Rancière and Alain Faure, in the beginning of their research on *La Parole ouvrière,* recuperate in the "tradition of the oppressed."[42]

5

Destructions?

We do not perceive the same things at all: depending on whether we widen our view to the *horizon* that extends beyond us, immense and immobile, or whether we focus our gaze on the *image* that passes by us, tiny and moving, right up close. The image is the *lucciola* of passing intermittences; the horizon bathes in the *luce* of definitive states, arrested times of totalitarianism or the finished times of the Last Judgment. Seeing the horizon, the beyond, means not seeing the images that come and brush against us. The little fireflies give form and glimmer to our fragile immanence; the "fierce spotlights" of the great light devour all form and all glimmer—all difference—in the transcendence of the final ends. Giving all our attention to the horizon means rendering ourselves incapable of looking at the slightest image.

Perhaps it is only in such moments of messianic exaltation that we may, eventually, find ourselves dreaming of a horizon that would fall away, that would render all images visible. This is what appears on rare occasions in the work of Walter Benjamin, when the topic is a very hypothetical history that has arrived at its end, where every *instant*—every image—can be seen summoned in the Last Judgment's absolute, paradoxical *duration*: "The chronicler who narrates events without distinguishing between major and minor ones acts in accord with the following truth: nothing that has ever happened should be regarded as lost for history. Of course only a redeemed mankind is granted the fullness of its past—which is to say, only for a redeemed mankind has its past become citable in all its moments. Each moment it has lived becomes a *citation à l'ordre du jour*. And that day is Judgment Day."[1]

But this "day" has not been given to us. What falls to us is only a "night," crossed here by the fireflies' soft flashes, there by the spotlights' cruel rays. Benjamin's theses, we know, are broken off—in words that are, for us, his very last—at the image of that messianic "small gateway" that holds "every second" of time invested by thought.[2] This narrow frame, this tiny lapse, designates nothing other, it seems to me, than the image itself: an image that "flashes up. . . . For it is an irretrievable image of the past which threatens to disappear in any present that does not recognize itself as intended in that image."[3] In the French version of his text, Benjamin writes that this definition of the image is based on "a verse from Dante" that no one, to my knowledge, has yet managed to identify.[4] But this memory, however vague, remains precious to us: Benjamin makes the image into something between Dante's Beatrice and Baude-laire's fleeting beauty [*fugitive beauté*], the ultimate *passante*.

The image would be the passing light that, like a comet, breaks through the immobility of all horizons: "The dialecti-cal image is an occurrence of ball lightning that runs across the whole horizon of the past," writes Benjamin in the very context—the "paralipomena" manuscripts—of his reflection on history and politics.[5] In this historical world that is our own—that is, far from any ultimate ending, from any Last Judgment—in our world where "this enemy has never ceased to be victorious"[6] and where the horizon seems hidden by the kingdom and its glory, the first political operator of protest, of crisis, of criticism or emancipation, must be called *image*, as that which is revealed as capable of *breaking through the horizon* of totalitarian constructions. Such is the meaning of a reflection—a crucial one, in my view—that Benjamin sketched out on the image's role as a way to "organize"—that is, to dismantle, to analyze, to contest—the very horizon of our basic pessimism:

> For to organize pessimism means . . . to discover in the space of political action . . . image space. This image space, however, can no longer be measured out by contemplation . . . the long-sought image space . . . , the world of universal and integral actuality.[7]

The image: a unique, precious apparition, even though it is such a very small thing, a thing that burns, a thing that falls.[8] Such is the "ball lightning" that Walter Benjamin evokes: it "runs across the whole horizon" only by falling toward us, *falling to us*. Only rarely does it rise toward the still sky of eternal ideas: generally it descends, it declines, it hurls itself and crashes into our earth, somewhere before or behind the horizon. Like a firefly, in the end, it disappears from our view, leaving us for a place where perhaps someone else will see it, somewhere else where its survival can still be seen. If, as we are trying to construct the hypothesis after Warburg and Benjamin, the image is the temporal operator of survivals—and in this role, bearer of a political power linked to our past as well as to our "integral actuality" and thus to our future—then we must commit ourselves to better understanding its *falling* movement toward us, that fall or that "decline," meaning that declination, which is not, whatever Pasolini may have feared in 1975, whatever Agamben may think today, a *disappearance*.

We must return, then, to the *horizon without recourse* that Agamben suggests in his liminary proposition in *Infancy and History*, to contrast it with this *recourse of the image* that we are here attempting to understand.[9] We have seen that Agamben views all of the contemporary from the perspective of a *destruction of experience* and bases his hypothesis on a reading of Benjamin: "experience has fallen."[10] For Agamben, this indeed means a *destruction that is accomplished, completed*: and it is this that "now makes everyday existence intolerable—as never before,"[11] even in the wartime moments he has just mentioned. Much as Pasolini saw an accomplished destruction in the disappearance of fireflies from his view, Agamben converts the "fall" that Benjamin diagnosed into a past result, into a "destruction" without recourse.

"The course of experience has fallen" *(die Erfahrund ist im Kurse gefallen)*: the participle *gefallen*, "fallen, declined," indicates, certainly, a terrible movement. But it is still a movement. Moreover, it sounds strange to our ear, because elsewhere the verb *gefallen* means the act of loving, pleasing, getting along. And above all, this movement does not concern experience itself but its "course" in the market of modern values (the "market of postmodern values" still confirms Benjamin's diagnosis). What Benjamin describes is doubtless an effective, efficient destruction; but it is an *unaccomplished,* perpetually incomplete destruction, its horizon never closed. It would be the same for experience as for the aura, then, for what is generally presented as the complete destruction of the aura in images in the time of their technological reproducibility should correctly be seen as what I have called a *supposition*: that which "falls" does not necessarily "disappear," and the images are still there, to reappear or shine through as some glimpse, vestige, or survival.

No doubt, all of Walter Benjamin's vocabulary in "The Storyteller" is a vocabulary of *decline*. But a decline perceived [*entendu*] with all its harmonics, with all the *recourses* implied in declination, inflection, the persistence of fallen things. From the beginning, Benjamin writes of the "decline of experience" in terms of a "phenomenon":[12] *Erscheinung*, meaning an apparition, precisely, an "apparition in spite of all," if I may. Next, he mentions a "process...which continues to this day":[13] a *Vorgang*, that is, a process, an event, a reaction (as the term is used in chemistry) or an *incident*, a word that describes exactly what Benjamin means by his reference to a falling movement and to the fact that this movement is not without consequence, without *incidence*.

A vocabulary of process, then. When Benjamin tells us that "the art of storytelling is coming to an end," he expresses in the same moment a horizon of "end" *(Ende)* and a movement without end *(neigen, "to lean, incline, lower")* that evokes not a thing that has disappeared but a thing that is "on the way to disappearance," rendered here by the verb *aussterben*, "to disperse, to fade out, to move toward disappearance."[14] It is, then, very much a question of "decline" and not of a completed disappearance: Benjamin uses the word *Niedergang*—often, as he does here—to indicate progressive descent, setting, the west (meaning the state of the sun, which disappears from our view yet does not cease to exist elsewhere, on the other side of the earth, below our feet, with the possibility, the "recourse," that it may reappear from the other side, in the east).

A little further on—I'm trying not to leave anything in shadow—Benjamin will write that "the art of storytelling has become rare,"[15] which certainly assumes a becoming *(Werden)* and not a mortal stasis, as well as the subsistence, however diminished, "rare," or "extraordinary" *(selten)*, of something that has therefore *not* been destroyed. The experience that the storyteller transmits "is coming to an end," but the verb used here, *gehen*, assumes that the end of the road—the horizon—is not yet planned for today.[16] It's this "coming" itself that should receive all of our attention. The last sentence of the essay—"The storyteller is the figure in which the righteous man encounters himself"[17]—is written in the *present* tense: not the intemporality of an eternal or absolute definition but the very temporality that, in our world today, in extreme precarity, is *surviving* and declining beneath the new forms of the decline itself.

The political and aesthetic urgency, then, in a period of "catastrophe"—this leitmotiv running through all of Benjamin's work—would be, not to carry the logical consequences of the decline up to its horizon of death, but instead to find the unexpected recourses from this decline in the quiet, secret space of images that still move there, like fireflies or isolated stars. We might remember the marvelous cosmological model that Lucretius proposed in *On the Nature of Things*: atoms "decline" perpetually, but their fall in this infinite *clinamen* allows exceptions with unforeseen consequences. An atom may diverge only slightly from its parallel trajectory, yet enough that it may collide with others, a collision from which a world may be born.[18] Such, then, would be the essential *recourse of decline*: bifurcation, collision, the "ball lightning" crossing the horizon, the invention of a new form. It's not at all surprising that Benjamin situated one of his great historiographic models in the thought of Alois Riegl, whose history of art aimed precisely to show the special vitality of these periods in so-called decline, such as late antiquity or—the period that concerns Benjamin in his work on the *Trauerspiel*—mannerism and baroque art.[19]

If we return to the text of "The Storyteller" with this perspective, we will soon find all the elements of that very vitality: it is the indestructible *imprint,* as "traces of the storyteller cling to a story the way the handprints of the potter cling to a clay vessel."[20] It is the epic *memory* whose transformation brings up, in modern novels—from Proust to surrealism—so many processes of remembrance *(Eingedenken)*.[21] It is the *intermittence* with which this memory reaches the reader today, despite his poverty of experience, as so many moments "when he is happy."[22] Using here the words *nur bisweilen,* "only occasionally,"

Benjamin gives us a precious clue about the temporal status of survivals. "That is why," he says about a story told by Herodotus in antiquity and still read today, "this story from ancient Egypt is still capable of provoking astonishment and reflection. It is like those seeds of grain that have lain for centuries in the airtight chambers of the pyramids and have retained their germinative power to this day."[23]

The course of experience has fallen, it's true. But it's up to us not to play that market. It's up to us to understand where and how this movement "at the same time is making it possible to find a new beauty in what is vanishing."[24] With acuity, with gravity, Agamben shows us an ultimate horizon for this *devaluation*. But, paradoxically, going too far in that direction means condemning oneself to making it only halfway down the necessary path. The "dialectical image" to which Benjamin calls us consists rather in bringing forth the *invaluable* moments that survive, that resist such an organization of values by exploding them with moments of surprise. Let us seek experiences that can still be transmitted, beyond all the "spectacles" bought and sold around us, beyond the performance of kingdoms and the light of glories. Are we "poor in experience"? Then let us make that poverty itself—that semidarkness—an experience. Adorno's passion for the work of Samuel Beckett[25] would certainly not be exempt from an implicit recourse to the precepts that Benjamin had already formulated in his 1936 essay on "The Storyteller."

The course of experience has fallen, but it is up to us, in each individual situation, to *raise that fall* up to dignity, to "new beauty," to a choreography, an invention of forms. In its fragility, in its firefly intermittence, doesn't the image take on this very power each time it shows its ability to reappear, to *survive*? In an article titled "The Immemorial Image," Agamben radicalizes the notion of the image by assigning it two fates, two horizons:

the first, one of *pure destruction* ("the image dies"); the second
is survival in Hades (the pagan version) or in apocatastasis,
the "final restoration" according to Origen of Alexandria (the
Christian version). In short, survival is understood here as the
afterlife—after death, after apocalypse, after end times—of *pure
redemption*.[26] Agamben adds that this very paradox—radical
passion and radical power—is "inscribed in the very origin of
Western metaphysics."[27] A way of lifting the image to the height
of metaphysics itself, albeit with Nietzsche and Heidegger as
artisans of its vertigo.

Walter Benjamin's proposition, which we will take up again
here, is entirely different: "to organize pessimism" in the historical world by discovering an "image space" in the very depths
of our "political action," as he says. This proposition concerns
the *impure temporality* of our historical life, which engages with
neither completed destruction nor the beginning of redemption.
And it's in this way that we must understand the survival of
images, their fundamental immanence: not their nothingness,
not their fullness, not their origins before all memory, not their
horizon after all catastrophe, but their recourse, the *recourse of
desire* and experience in the depth of our most immediate deci-
sions, our most banal everyday life.

From 1933 to 1940, at the very time that Walter Benjamin was discussing this possibility of "organizing pessimism"
through recourse to certain images or alternative configurations
of thought, his everyday life certainly offered him little rest.
Can we even imagine what life was like for him, as a German
Jew "without recourse," in constant flight as the trap closed in
around him? Agamben's description of the destruction of experience in an "everyday existence" that has become "intolerable—
as never before"[28] must be softened in light of this contrast. A
contrast all the greater because Benjamin was able to "organize
his pessimism" with the grace of fireflies, seeking—between

Bertolt Brecht's epic theater and the surrealist poets' urban wanderings, for example, or between the Bibliothèque nationale de France and the Passage des Panoramas—an "image space" that could counter the policing—the terrible constraints—of his life. The course of experience had fallen, but Benjamin answered it with *thought images* and by *image experiments,* of which the texts on hashish, among others, still offer some striking examples by their recourse of a "genuine aura" or an *infancy of the gaze* on all things.[29]

Agamben has proclaimed the destruction of experience and mourning for all infancy, as Pasolini did the disappearance of the fireflies, projecting onto the present what he knew of various world war situations, notably those that Benjamin described. And yet, the experience of war teaches us—by the fact that this experience found the conditions, however fragile, of its narration and its transmission—that pessimism was sometimes "organized" to the point of producing, by its very performance, the intermittent flash and hope of fireflies. A flash to make *words appear freely,* at a time when words seemed taken captive by a situation with no way out. We might think about the collection of texts that Henri Michaux composed between 1940 and 1944, under the title *Ordeals, Exorcisms*: "Their reason for being," he wrote in the opening: "to hold back the surrounding forces of a hostile world."[30] We might think about the admirable *Hypnos* notebooks that René Char wrote during his daily struggles in the Maquis, in which the political resistance—active, military, in constant mortal danger—joined forces with what we see here as "resistance" of thought.[31] We might think about Victor Klemperer's *LTI,* that "act of self-defense, an SOS sent to myself," as he wrote at the start, from the space of everyday oppression: work in which the *elucidation of language* became, in the necessary shadows of clandestine activity, the "firefly-words" riposte to the fierce "spotlight-words" imposed by Nazi propaganda.[32]

It has even happened that the darkest words are not words of absolute disappearance but those of a survival *in spite of all*, written from the depths of hell. "Firefly-words," again, from the newspapers of the Warsaw ghetto and the chronicle of its insurrection; "firefly-words" from the manuscripts of Sonderkommando members, hidden in the ashes of Auschwitz, whose "flash" holds the sovereign desire of its narrator, he who wanted to tell, to bear witness from beyond his own death.[33] Between the pitiless shadows of the gas chambers and the blinding sunlight in the summer of 1944, these resistants in the Sonderkommando even managed to make *images appear* when imagination seemed clouded by a reality too overwhelming to be thought.[34] Clandestine images, of course, long hidden, long useless, but images transmitted to us, anonymously, in what Benjamin recognized as the ultimate authority [*sanction*] of every story, every testimony of experience—that is, the *authority of the dying*.[35]

6

Images

"No one dies so poor that he leaves nothing behind": in this dictum from Pascal, which Benjamin cites,[1] one should manage to find the strength to see the slightest sketch of a butterfly on yellowed paper—found in the Terezin concentration camp, drawn by Marika Friedmanova at the age of eleven, just before she was deported and gassed in Auschwitz—as a precious, surviving legacy.[2] Even dreams, those puzzles hidden in the deepest depths, can come to us—in glimpses, of course, in intermittent flashes—as so many "firefly-images." This is the quixotic task that Charlotte Beradt undertook, her Benjaminian storyteller's task: she recounts how in 1933, terrified by the turn that events were taking in Germany, she began to have recurring anxiety dreams: "I awoke [one morning] bathed in perspiration, my teeth clenched. Once again, as on countless previous nights, I had been hunted from pillar to post in a dream—shot at, tortured, scalped. But on this night, of all nights, the thought occurred to me that I might not be the only one among thousands upon thousands to be condemned to such dreams by the dictatorship."[3]

At that moment, which marked her decision to record the dreams of those around her, Charlotte Beradt rose to the status of a "storyteller" in the sense that, Benjamin says, "a great storyteller will always be rooted in the people. . . . All great

storytellers have in common the freedom with which they
climb up or down the rungs of their experience, as if on a ladder. A ladder extended downward to the interior of the earth
and disappearing into the clouds: this is the image for a collective experience to which even the deepest shock in every
individual experience—death—constitutes no impediment
or barrier."⁴ In this manner, from 1933 and 1939—the date of
her flight from Germany—Charlotte Beraldt gathered a whole
corpus of dreams, with the goal of offering something like a
psychic document of totalitarianism, of political terror as a
haunted (haunting) process at the deepest level of the soul.
An extraordinary collection, this "oneiric inquiry" was carried
out with around three hundred people. It explains nothing,
neither the nature of Nazism nor the psychology of dreams,
but as Charlotte Beradt said herself, it provides an intimate
"seismography" of the political history of the Third Reich. "It
had occurred to me from time to time that a record should be
kept of such dreams. . . . They might one day serve as evidence
when the time came to pass judgment on National Socialism as
a historical phenomenon, for they seemed to reveal a great deal
about people's deepest feelings and reactions as they became
part of the mechanism of totalitarianism."⁵

We can understand, then, how an *inner experience,* the most
"subjective," the most "obscure" there is, may appear as a *flash
for another,* from the moment that it finds the right form of
its construction, its narration, its transmission. The dreams
that Beradt gathered transform reality, of course; but that very
transformation holds the value of clandestine knowledge, exactly at the point where a threat, of being *represented* [*figuré*],
serves as an anthropological diagnosis, a political prophecy, as a
heterotopic—but also "hyperaesthetic"—knowledge of the time
lived in the day through the images dreamed at night. Knowledge of hard times, times of lead (the hypocrites' heavy cloaks,

the material of killing projectiles, the color of melancholia): "Am going to bury myself in lead. Tongue is already leaden, locked in fear. Fear will go away when I'm all covered with lead. Will lie immobile, shot full of lead. When they come, I'll say, 'The leaden cannot rise up.'"[6]

Firefly-knowledge. Clandestine knowledge, hieroglyphs, realities constantly submitted to censorship: "I dreamt that I no longer dream about anything but rectangles, triangles and octagons, all of which somehow look like Christmas cookies—you see, it was forbidden to dream."[7] Knowledge of a humanity as disposable as paper in a wastebasket, or even worse (the dreamer was Jewish): "Two benches were standing side by side in Tiergarten Park, one painted the usual green and the other yellow [in those days, Jews were permitted to sit only on specially painted yellow benches]. There was a trash can between them. I sat down on the trash can and hung a sign around my neck like the one blind beggars sometimes wear—also like those the government makes 'race violators' wear. It read, '*I Make Room for Trash If Need Be.*'"[8] And even knowledge of the atrocities committed, from a dreamer who knew nothing as yet of the reality of the camps: "I dreamt I was being forced to list all known inhuman punishments. I made them up in my dream. Then I got even by screaming, 'All enemies have to die!'"[9]

In his afterword to the German edition of Charlotte Beradt's book, the historian Reinhart Koselleck made a remarkable comment on the paradox of a collection of psychic *fictions* that, manifestly, "rather than offering a realistic representation of reality, ... instead throw a particularly glaring light on the very reality from which they come."[10] It might be more accurate to say that the *light* in question is not "glaring" but strange—striped with dark shadows, too close or too far to render its object clearly visible—and, most of all, intermittent. The important thing here is that the historian recognizes in the dream *story* an authority in historical *knowledge* as such. Not by chance, Koselleck then mentions Kleist, Hebbel, and Kafka, meaning three "storytellers" who are paradigmatic of the concept that Walter Benjamin set forth.[11] It is then, he says, that "the facticity... gains a multilayeredness in which the epistemological work of dreams is contained."[12] The images dreamed *under* the terror then become images produced *on* the terror. "A common signature of the dreams collected by Beradt is that they make known a truth which is concealed in reality but has not yet become empirically intelligible."[13]

Which is why "firefly-images" can be seen not only as *testimony* but also as prophecies, *previsions* about the political history in the process of becoming: "For a historian working on the history of the Third Reich, Beradt's documentation of dreams represents a first-rate source. It opens up layers not even reached by diary entries. The narrated dreams...lead us into the recesses of the apparently private realm of the everyday, to where waves of propaganda and terror penetrate. The dreams bear witness to an initially open terror that then turns insidious, and they even anticipate its violent crescendo."[14] If it's true, as Pierre Fédida says, that "the dream has made contact with the dead" in its fundamental metapsychological constitution, if it's true that "it is the touch of the dead that makes the dream visionary,"[15] then we can understand this *seeing*, reconfigured here by glimpses in the dream narratives, under the *authority of the dying* that Benjamin considered the ultimate paradigm of all transmitted experience. But the dying person is not always the agonized, the voiceless, the "*Muselmann*," as Agamben describes. Dying—we all are, at every moment, if only we face the temporal condition, the extreme fragility, of our "flashes" of life. "We all die *incessantly*," wrote Georges Bataille, in the time of the Second World War. And he added, "The brief time that separates us from the void has the inconsistency of a dream."[16]

It would take another whole book to understand exactly what formed, in Georges Bataille during wartime, this combination of a *retreat into darkness* and the "will to chance," as he said, meaning the sovereign will, anxious and frenetic, that drove him to throw so many signals into the night, like a firefly trying to escape the flame of spotlights, the better to *emit his flashes* of thoughts, poetry, desires, stories—to transmit at any cost.

The text that he decided to undertake, at the beginning of the war, was titled *Guilty*. Its first chapter, "Night," starts, "The date I begin writing (5 September 1939) is not a coincidence. I begin because of the events, but not to speak of them."[17] Paradox, crack of nonknowledge, sovereignty far from any kingdom: not speaking of events the better to respond to them, the better to oppose them with desire (his flash in the night), knowing very well that this desire was nothing but cracks, fragilities, the intermittence of the dying, between "decline" [*déchéance*] and what he wanted so badly, still, to call "glory": "There is no being without a crack, but we go from enduring the crack, the degradation, to glory"—adding a condition, to distance himself from any prestige or any religious path: "Christianity attains glory by escaping what is (humanly) glorious."[18] Far from the kingdom and the light, then, Bataille was trying to send his signals through the night like so many paradoxes, of which the result, as we know, would be called *Inner Experience*.[19]

In the meantime, under his pseudonym with the aptly named Éditions du Solitaire, Bataille published his scandalous *Madame Edwarda*, a story in which we understand that *erotic experience* would perhaps offer a first response of the "guilty" to the deadly events dominating all of Europe. It's a dance of desire in the Parisian night, a countersubject to the movements of airplanes and the fierce spotlights of the ongoing war. Just like the young Pasolini around the same time in a forest clearing near Bologna, the narrator of *Madame Edwarda* strips naked "in those streets—the propitious ones—which run between the Boulevard Poissonière and the Rue Saint-Denis." The prostitute that he meets then—a *lucciola,* not in the normal sense but, if I may, in the "dirty sense"—will appear and disappear in the intermittence of her light ("hairy and pink, just as full of life as some loathsome squid") and of her darkness ("She was entirely black, simply there, as distressing as an emptiness, a hole"). She will twist like a worm, "flop like a fish" in a spasm of white nudity, like a glowworm. To fall asleep in the night, suddenly, and to evaporate from the story, just as fireflies can so easily disappear from our view.[20]

Around this time, Bataille met Maurice Blanchot, who had just published *Thomas the Obscure.* At the home of Denise Rollin in autumn 1941, he tried to reconstitute something like a community of fireflies—gatherings of a "Socratic school" where he would read fragments from *Inner Experience* as he was writing it—but in "the absence of salvation, in the renunciation of all hope," since that experience, for him, could "only be a contestation of itself and nonknowledge."[21] In 1942, he contracted pulmonary tuberculosis, for a period of suffering that, as Michel Surya says, must have "concentrated Bataille's solitude a little more."[22] In retreat at a village in Normandy, Bataille wrote bursts of poems such as *The Dead Man,* a short narrative about a frightening erotic experience whose preface was planned to include terrible visions—lived ones—of the war in progress: the broken German plane, flames, formless and blackened faces, and that foot, "the one human thing belonging to any of the bodies" resting intact among the ruins.[23]

Throughout this entire period, the writing of *Guilty* was an attempt to create something like a collision between the immense space of "the miseries of the present" and the infinitely restricted space of "chance," of the luminous laugh, of "unemployed negativity."[24] Later, *Inner Experience* would attempt to understand the "voyage to the end of the possible of man," even if that man may be given up to the kingdom of war and destruction.[25] In this sense, experience is a crack, nonknowledge, test of the unknown, lack of plan, wandering in shadows.[26] It is the ultimate in *powerlessness* [*l'impouvoir*], especially in relation to the kingdom and its glory. But it is a *power* [*puissance*]—Nietzsche haunts this whole vocabulary—of an entirely different order: a power of contestation, Bataille says. "I contest in the name of contestation what experience itself is (the will to proceed to the end of the possible). Experience, its authority, its method, do not distinguish themselves from the contestation."[27]

The course of experience has fallen, no doubt. But the fall is still an experience—that is, a contestation in its very movement—of the fall undergone. The fall, nonknowledge: these become forces in the writing that transmits them. "Impotence [*l'impuissance*] cries out within me," Bataille writes, no doubt.[28] But this cry—if he manages, if he emits his signal, his flash—is the power of contestation. Silence is also weakness, yet "the refusal to communicate is a more hostile means of communication, but the most powerful."[29] It's very significant that Bataille offers some examples of this power that correspond to what Walter Benjamin hoped for from images, specifically, *luminous bodies passing in the night.* Balls of lightning crossing the horizon, comets that appear, go elsewhere, and become lost. Fireflies, in a way, more or less quiet. More or less close to us in the night. "A man is a particle inserted in unstable and tangled groups," Bataille writes again, "a stopping-point favoring a resurgence"; but a stopping-point bearing energy, capable of bursting out: "an inflamed gushing forth, *overpowering*, even free of its own convulsion. A character of dance and of decomposing agility."[30]

Experience is to knowledge as a dance in the darkest night is to stasis in stilled light. Yet in the night, still capable of finding *unexpected flashes,* neither gaze nor desire ceases: the subject of experience, Bataille affirms, "is a spectator, it is eyes which seek out the point, or at least, in this operation visual existence is condensed in the eyes. This character does not cease if night falls. What is thereby found in deep obscurity is a keen desire to see when, in the face of this desire, everything slips away. But the desire for existence thus dissipated into night turns to an object of ecstasy."[31] A flickery object, an *intermittent spectacle,* it goes without saying, as our own eyelids open and close: "My eyes are open, it is true, but it would have been necessary not to say it, to remain frozen like an animal. I wanted to speak, and, as if the words bore the weight of a thousand slumbers, gently, as if appearing not to see, my eyes closed."[32] (Then they open again, we know, so that the author of *Inner Experience* may write this very page, perhaps in the night, by lamplight, on a sheet of white paper.)

This is the context in which Bataille, at the end of the war, returns to philosophical contestation and to the construction of an *other knowledge*—what he will name "atheology" here, "heterology" there—capable of resituating himself, of again staking out a position in the political history of his present time. "Written in a rush" during the German retreat of 1944 (the centenary of the philosopher),[33] published in February 1945, *On Nietzsche* is an extraordinary book. It blends an erratic war journal—that is, the *nonknowledge* of an experience, a disorienting blend of aerial bombardments with sideshows, tragic ruins, and children's games[34]—with an attempt at conceptual *elucidation* intended to restore a use value to Nietzsche's writings beyond their usage by the fascists, of which Bataille constructs, yet again, the most blistering critique.[35]

And it is once again an experience in tension between loss and ecstasy, *shadows and luminosities,* that will be described in these pages. The book opens with a quotation from Nietzsche, translated as "I only just barely prevent my flame from bursting from my body."[36] Later the question is one of a "moving vista," toward something like a "solar explosion": "With even the smallest possible bet, I open a perspective raising the ante infinitely. *In this moving vista, a summit can be glimpsed. As the highest point—the most intense degree—of attraction for itself, that can define life. A kind of solar explosion, independent of consequences.*"[37] In the end, it's a matter of affirming that thought *at the level of experience* is something like a ball of fire or a firefly, wonderful and disappearing: "Nietzsche's doctrines are strange in this way: in that one cannot follow them. They put imprecise, often dazzling hints in front of us: no path leads in the indicated direction."[38]

None of this prevented Bataille from staking out his position, after the hostilities ended, in order to recall where the "tragedy" of the world war had started, that is, the Spanish Civil War, where "fascism's last sanctuary" held under the reign of Franco.[39] As he was editing a journal titled *Actualité* that was specially dedicated to "Free Spain"—which collected texts from Albert Camus, Jean Cassou, Federico García Lorca, Maurice Blanchot, and Ernest Hemingway, among others—Georges Bataille rediscovered the political meaning of all experience, describing its complexity by tying together, in his own text, Goya's *Tres de Mayo,* the death of Granero in the Madrid arena, the "culture of anguish" inherent in the *cante jondo,* and the "intimate liberty" of Andalusian anarchists. Even if they were locked up in Franco's jails, with only a cigarette's ember for light in the darkness and the heartrending call of their songs, called *carceleras.*[40]

So we must not say that experience, at whatever moment in history, has been "destroyed." On the contrary—and no matter how powerful the kingdom and its glory, no matter how

universally efficient the "society of the spectacle"—we must
affirm that *experience is indestructible,* even when it may well
become reduced to survivals and clandestine moments, to
simple glimmers in the night. In Agamben's pessimism, there
may be a relationship to establish between his thesis on "the
destruction of experience"—his mourning for all infancy, since
1978—and the definition of peoples that he would finally bor-
row from Carl Schmitt in 2008. If one of the most beautiful of
Agamben's books remains, to my eyes, *The Coming Community,*
that's because it seems written to open up a field of recourse: a
book on "whatever being" as *lovable,* or on the human face as
that which "passes from the common to the proper and from
the proper to the common" as this passage opens up the space
of an *ethos.*[41] But in the end, it does not escape the Heideggerian "irreparable" or the question, offensive to my eyes, of the
"Kingdom of the Messiah,"[42] which is still a kingdom.

Isn't it necessary to search first among the *communities that
remain*—without reigning—the very recourse, the open space
of answers to our questions? Kingdoms, "governmentalities,"
as Foucault says, or "the police" according to Rancière, certainly
tend to reduce or subjugate peoples. But that reduction, even in
extreme cases like genocide, is almost never without remnants,
and remnants almost never exist without moving: fleeing, hid-
ing, burying evidence, going elsewhere, finding a way out—this
is what we learn from the free "inner experiences" that Bataille
wrote about, or Victor Klemperer's language experiments, or
Charlotte Beradt's transmitted dreams. Or even those "messages
in a bottle," desperate but addressed, agonizing but precise,
from members of the Sonderkommando at Auschwitz.

All of these clandestine experiences are addressed—an address all the more urgent because impeded at first—to peoples
who can or are willing, at some time or another, to understand
them. All are political acts, founded in the "community that

remains." All have "roots among the people," as Walter Benjamin recognized in every story capable of transmitting an experience to another person. It's not the fact that Robert Antelme came back from the concentration camp alive that suggested the idea of the *indestructible* to Maurice Blanchot. Rather, it was the fact that Antelme's book, *The Human Race,* in its status as a text addressed to the species, a transmitted story, was a literal manifestation—and as with Primo Levi's *Survival in Auschwitz,* I cannot bring myself to imagine that one day, it will not be read by anyone—of this power: that "man is indestructible and he can nonetheless be destroyed,"[43] a paradox that can be understood, obviously, with the idea of *survival.* Survival of signs or images when the survival of the protagonists themselves is not assured. And yet that power is a beginning, as Blanchot says again, "the point of departure for a *common demand,*" founded on the act "to entitle speech" of a people's experience in the forms of its transmission.[44]

Such a resistance of thought, of signs and images against the "destruction of experience"—when it is not simply against destruction—perhaps nobody has expressed better than Hannah Arendt this paradoxical recourse, this *freedom to make peoples appear* in spite of all, in spite of the kingdom's censors and the glory's blinding lights (that is, when the kingdom plunges everything into darkness or when the glory only uses its light to blind us more fully). In her elegy to Lessing, titled "On Humanity in Dark Times," Arendt discusses the situation of one confronted with such a time, when "the public realm has lost its power of illumination,"[45] when we no longer feel "enlightened" according to the order of reasons nor "radiant" according to the order of affects.

Here, then, is what a few people in such situations have chosen to do: "retreat from the world" of *light,* all the while working on something that may "be useful to the world again"[46]—a flash, a *glimmer,* in other words. To retreat without withdrawing, like Lessing, who remained "radically critical and, in respect to the public realm of his time, completely revolutionary" even in his solitude: "Lessing retreated into thought, but not at all into his own self; and if for him a secret link between thought and action did exist . . . , the link consisted in the fact that both action and thought occur in the form of movement and that, therefore, freedom underlies both: *freedom of movement.*"[47] In this way, the suffering inherent in withdrawal becomes the joy inherent in movement, this desire, this *acting in spite of all* capable of making meaning in its transmission to another: "The meaning of a committed act," writes Arendt, following in a straight line from Benjamin, "is revealed only when the action itself has come to an end and become a story susceptible to narration."[48]

And here is how "a bit of humanness in a world become inhuman had been achieved."[49] In the lovely text that begins *Between Past and Present,* titled "The Gap between Past and Future," Arendt returns to the examples of René Char and Franz Kafka in the hope that their most invaluable lessons on this "age-old treasure which, under the most varied circumstances, appears abruptly, unexpectedly, and disappears again, under different mysterious conditions," will be transmitted, somewhere in the open gap between memory and desire.[50] Again, memory must be "a force, and not . . . a burden."[51] Again, we must recognize the essential vitality of survivals and of memory in general when it finds the right forms for its transmission. Then what will emerge, in that geometric combination of retreat and nonwithdrawal, is what Arendt calls a *diagonal force,* which differs from the two forces—that of the past, that of the future—from which it nevertheless results. "The two antagonistic forces are both unlimited as to their origins, the one coming from an infinite past and the other from an infinite future; but though they have no known beginning, they have a terminal ending, the point at which they clash. The diagonal force, on the contrary, would be limited as to its origin, its starting point being the clash of the antagonistic forces, but it would be infinite with respect to its ending by virtue of having resulted from the concerted action of two forces whose origin is infinity. This diagonal force, whose origin is known, whose direction is determined by past and future, but whose eventual end lies in infinity, is the perfect metaphor for the activity of thought."[52]

Such is the fireflies' infinite recourse: their retreat when there is no withdrawal but a "diagonal force"; their clandestine community of "particles of humanity," those signals sent now and then, intermittently; their essential freedom of movement; their ability to make desire appear as the ultimate indestructible (and here I'm reminded of the very last words that Freud chose for his *Interpretation of Dreams*: "This future, taken by the dreamer as present, has been formed into the likeness of that past by the indestructible wish"[53]). The fireflies: it's up to us not to see them disappear. We, ourselves, must assume their freedom of movement, the retreat without withdrawal, the diagonal force, the ability to make particles of humanity appear, to make the indestructible desire appear. We must, ourselves—in retreat from the kingdom and the glory, in the open gap between the past and the future—become fireflies and thus form again a community of desire, a community of flashes shining out, of dances in spite of all, of thoughts to transmit. To say *yes* to the night all crossed with glimmers and flashes, and not be content merely to describe the *no* of the light that blinds us.

We do not live in one world but between two worlds, at least. The first is inundated with light, the second crossed with flashes. At the center of the light, we're supposed to believe, twist and turn those few who today are called, with a cruel Hollywood antiphrase, the *People,* or sometimes the *stars*—the stars, we know, carry divine names[54]—and we gorge ourselves with mostly useless information about them. Smoke and mirrors, part of the system of the "kingdom's" effective glory: the glory demands only one thing from us, and that's our unanimous acclamation. But making their way along the margins, across an infinitely more extensive territory, are innumerable peoples about whom we know too little and for whom counter-information seems ever more necessary. *Firefly-peoples,* when they retreat into the night, seek their freedom of movement as they can, flee the spotlights of the "kingdom," do the impossible to affirm their desires, to emit their own flashes and send their signals to others. Suddenly I'm reminded—this is only a recent example; there are many others I could mention—of the few, fragile images flashing through the night at the Sangatte camp, in 2002, in Laura Waddington's film titled *Border.*[55]

Laura Waddington spent several months in the areas surrounding the Red Cross camp at Sangatte. She filmed Afghani and Iraqi refugees who were trying desperately to escape the police and to cross through the Channel Tunnel to reach England. Of all this, she could get only *firefly-images*: images on the brink of disappearance, always altered by the urgency of their flight, always close to those who, to fulfill their plans, hide in the night and attempt the impossible, risking their lives. The "diagonal force" of this film comes at the cost of clarity, of course: the need for lightweight equipment, the shutter at maximum, impure images, uncertain focus, invasive graininess, jerky rhythms that produce something like a slow-motion effect. Flash-images, even so. We can see only a little, only glimpses: bodies positioned in the ditch below a highway, beings crossing through the night toward an impossible horizon. Despite the overpowering darkness, these are not bodies rendered invisible but rather "particles of humanity" that the film manages precisely to *make appear,* however fragile and brief those apparitions may be.

What appears in these bodies in flight is nothing other than the persistence of a plan, the indestructible character of a desire. What appears is also, sometimes, grace: the grace contained in any desire that takes form. Gratuitous and unexpected beauty, as when a Kurdish refugee dances in the night, in the wind, with only his blanket for covering: this vestment for his dignity, and, somehow, for his fundamental joy, his joy in spite of all (see Figure 2). *Border* is an illegal film, crossed with all the *states of light*. On one hand, there are those glimmers in the night: infinitely precious, because they carry freedom, but also agonizing, because they are always subject to a palpable danger. On the other hand—as in the situation that Pasolini described in 1941—we see the "fierce spotlights" of the kingdom, if not the glory: beams [*faisceaux*] from police flashlights across the countryside, the implacable ray of light that sweeps from a helicopter, through the ambient shadows. Even the simple lights of houses, the streetlamps or headlights that pass on the highway, grip us by the throat, because of the painful—visually painful—contrast with all that humanity thrown into the night, thrown again into flight.

These contrasts of the states of light correspond to a striking contrast of sound in which two *states of voice* give Waddington's narrative all its dialectical subtlety, despite the extreme simplicity of her formal choices. There is the voice of the artist herself: the voice of a very young woman, musical although artless, with an extraordinary tenderness. Modestly, she carries out the necessary work of the witness: she tells us her story as well as its intrinsic limits; she does not judge or dominate the story that she tells; she speaks to individual beings, people she has met and names specifically (Omar, Abdullah, Mohamed), without omitting the frightening perspective of the whole phenomenon (about sixty thousand refugees would come through Sangatte, we learn).

Figure 2. Laura Waddington, *Border,* 2004.

When we spectators sometimes feel dazzled by an overexposed shot, Waddington tells us how the refugees themselves would return to camp blinded by tear gas.

Suddenly, in the midst of her narration and her voice—which reminds me not a little of the plaintive lyrics that the poet Forough Farrokhzad recited to accompany *The House Is Black,* her uncompromising documentary on an Iranian leper colony—explodes a sequence of live sound recordings, filmed from within the refugees' protest against the imminent closure of the camp. Here we see not glimmers but explosions, flairs; these are no longer speeches but cries, yelled out at full force, to no avail. The camera itself protests and struggles. The image of all this is fumbled, in danger: it tries with every shot to save itself. Later the silence will gather again. We will see a group of refugees—but now we must not say "refugees"; instead we must say "fugitives"—guided by a smuggler, moving away through the shadows toward a vaguely luminous horizon. Their goal is over there, beyond, behind that line. Even if we know very well that "over there" will still not be a refuge for them. In the end, they blend into the darkness of underbrush and the line of the horizon. Headlights still shine out. The film ends on something like a halt in dazzlement.

Images, then, to organize our pessimism. Images to protest against the kingdom's glory and its beams of hard light. Have the fireflies disappeared? Of course not. Some of them are very near to us—they brush against us in the night; others have gone elsewhere, beyond the horizon, trying to reform their community, their minority, their shared desire. Even here, Waddington's images remain, as well as the names—in the closing credits—of all those people she met. We can watch the film again, we can show it, and circulate glimpses, which will spark others: firefly-images.

Notes

1. Hells?

1 Dante Alighieri, *The Inferno,* trans. Mark Musa (Bloomington: Indiana University Press, 1995), XXVI:25–32, 189–90.

2 Alighieri, XXVI:42, 190.

3 Sandro Botticelli, *Drawings for Dante's "Divine Comedy"* (London: Royal Academy of Arts, 2000), 108–9.

4 Pliny the Elder, *Natural History,* trans. John Bostock (London: Taylor and Francis, 1855), XI:42.

5 See, notably, Pierre Lemonnier, *Le Sabbat des lucioles: Sorcellerie, chamanisme et imaginaire cannibale en Nouvelle-Guinée* (Paris: Stock, 2006).

6 Erich Auerbach, *Dante: Poet of the Secular World,* trans. Michael Dirda (New York: New York Review of Books, 2007).

7 R. Longhi, "Gli affreschi del Carmine, Masaccio e Dante," in *Opere complete, VIII-1: Fatti di Masolino e di Masaccio e altri studi sul Quattrocento, 1910–1967* (Florence: Sansoni, 1975), 67–70. See also Pier Paolo Pasolini, "Qu'est-ce qu'un maître?" and "Sur Roberto Longhi," in *Écrits sur la peinture,* trans. H. Joubert-Laurencin (Paris: Carré, 1997), 77–86.

8 See Nico Naldini, introduction to *The Letters of Pier Paolo Pasolini, vol. 1, 1940–1954,* by Pier Paolo Pasolini, trans. Stuart Hood, ed. Nico Naldini (London: Quartet Books, 1992), 17.

9 Pasolini, *Letters,* 1:121.

10   Pasolini.

11   Pasolini.

12   Pasolini, 121–22.

13   Pasolini, 122. [Brackets in Stuart Hood's translation.—T.N.]

14   Pier Paolo Pasolini, "The Sequence of the Paper Flower,"
     in *Love and Anger*, cited in David Ward, *A Poetics of Resistance* (Cranbury, N.J.: Associated University Presses, 1995),
     146.

15   Jean-Paul Cunier, "La disparition des lucioles," *Lignes* 18 (2005):
     72.

16   Pier Paolo Pasolini, "L'articulo delle lucciole," in *Saggi sulla
     politica e sulla società*, ed. W. Siti and S. De Laude (Milan:
     Arnoldo Mondadori, 1999), 404–11; also in *Scritti corsari* (Milan: Garzanti, 1977). "Disappearance of the Fireflies," trans.
     Christopher Mott, in *Diagonal Thoughts*, ed. Stoffel Debuysere (Brussels, June 23, 2014), http://www.diagonalthoughts
     .com/?p=2107.

17   On the tradition of "infamous images," see Gherardo Ortalli,
     La pittura infamante nei secoli XIII–XVI (Rome: Società Editoriale Jouvence, 1979). S. Y. Edgerton, *Pictures and Punishment:
     Art and Criminal Prosecution during the Florentine Renaissance*
     (Ithaca, N.Y.: Cornell University Press, 1985). In *La Rabbia*,
     Pasolini lingers on a torture scene of this kind.

18   Pasolini, "Disappearance of the Fireflies."

19   Pasolini.

20   Pasolini.

21   Pasolini.

22   Pasolini.

23   Pier Paolo Pasolini, "D'un fascisme à l'autre," in *Entretiens
     avec Jean Duflot* (Paris: Gutenberg, 2007), 173–83.

24   Pier Paolo Pasolini, "Acculturation et acculturation," in *Écrits
     corsaires*, trans. French by P. Guilhon (Paris: Flammarion,
     2005), 49.

25 Pier Paolo Pasolini, "Le veritable fascisme," in *Écrits corsaires,* 76–82.

26 Pier Paolo Pasolini, "Le génocide," in *Écrits corsaires,* 261.

27 Pier Paolo Pasolini, "We're All in Danger," interview with Furio Colombo, trans. Pasquale Verdicchio, in *In Danger,* ed. Jack Hirschman (San Francisco: City Lights, 2010), 235.

28 Pasolini, "Disappearance of the Fireflies."

29 Pier Paolo Pasolini, *La meglio gioventù: Poesie friulane* (1941–1953), *Tutte le poesie,* ed. Walter Siti (Milan: Arnoldo Mondadori, 2003); Pasolini, "La poesia dialettale del Novecento," in *Saggi sulla letturatura e sull'arte,* ed. W. Siti and S. De Laude (Milan: Arnoldo Mondadori, 1999), 713–857; Pasolini, "La poesia popolare italiana," in *Saggi sulla letturatura e sull'arte,* 859–993. See also K. von Hofer, *Funktionen des Dialekts in der italianischen Gegenwartsliteratur: Pier Paolo Pasolini* (Munich: Wilhelm Fink, 1971); M. Teodonio, ed., *Pasolono tra friulano e romanesco* (Rome: Centro Studi Giuseppe Gioachino Belli-Editore Colombo, 1997); F. Cadel, *La lingua dei desideri: Il dialetto secondo Pier Paolo Pasolini* (Lecce, Italy: Piero Manni, 2002).

30 Pier Paolo Pasolini, *Stories from the City of God,* trans. Marina Harss (New York: Handsel Books, 2003); Pasolini, *The Long Road of Sand* (London: Contrasto Books, 2015).

31 See, notably, E. Siciliano, ed., *Pasolini e Roma* (Rome-Cinisello Balsamo: Museo di Roma in Trastavere-Silvana Editoriale, 2005).

32 Pier Paolo Pasolini, "Les gens cultivés et la culture populaire," in *Écrits corsaires,* 235–236; see also Pasolini, "Étroitesse de l'histoire et immensité du monde paysan," in *Écrits corsaires,* 83–88.

33 Pasolini, "We're All in Danger," 239.

34 See, notably, Adelio Ferrerro, "La ricerca dei popoli perduti e il presente come orrore," in *Il cinema di Pier Paolo Pasolini*

(Venice: Marsilio Editori, 1977), 109–55; see also R. Schérer, "L'alliance de l'archaïque et de la révolution," in *Passages Pasoliniens* (Villeneuve d'Ascq: Presses Universitaires du Septentrion, 2006), 17–30.

35   Pier Paolo Pasolini, *Lutheran Letters,* trans. Stuart Hood (Manchester, U.K.: Carcanet New Press, 1987), 35–36.

36   Walter Benjamin, "The Work of Art in the Age of Its Technological Reproducibility," in *"The Work of Art in the Age of Its Technological Reproducibility" and Other Writings on Media,* ed. Michael W. Jennings (Cambridge, Mass.: Belknap Press of Harvard University Press, 2008), 49n24.

37   Guy Debord, *The Society of the Spectacle,* trans. Donald Nicholson-Smith (New York: Zone Books, 2012), 15–16.

38   Pier Paolo Pasolini, "Néo-capitalisme télévisuel," trans. to French by C. Michel and H. Joubert-Laurencin, in *Contre la télévision* (Besançon: Les Solitaires intempestifs, 2003), 22.

39   Pasolini, "Disappearance of the Fireflies."

40   Pasolini.

41   Cunier, "Disparition des lucioles," 78–79.

42   Alain Brossat, "De l'inconvénient d'être prophète dans un monde cynique et désenchanté," *Lignes* 18 (2005): 47–48.

43   Brossat, 62.

2. Survivals

1   Denis Roche, *La Disparition des lucioles (réflexions sur l'acte photographique)* (Paris: l'Étoile, 1982).

2   Roche, 158 (where Pasolini's death is spontaneously mentioned).

3   Walter Benjamin, "Paris, Capital of the Nineteenth Century," in *The Arcades Project,* trans. Howard Eiland and Kevin McLaughlin (Cambridge, Mass.: Belknap Press of Harvard University Press, 1999), 3–26. See also Georges Didi-Huberman, *Ce que nous voyons, ce qui nous regarde* (Paris: Minuit, 1992), 53–152,

and Didi-Huberman, *Confronting Images: Questioning the Ends of a Certain History of Art,* trans. John Goodman (University Park: Pennsylvania State University Press, 2005).

4   Roche, *La Disparition des lucioles,* 165.

5   Roche, 166.

6   Roche, 149–50.

7   M. Samuel-Rousseau, *Les Lucioles de la Villa Médicis* (Paris: J. Hamelle, [1917]).

8   See F. A. McDermot, *Coleopterum Catalogus, Supplementa IX, Lampyridae,* dir. W. O. Steel (The Hague: W. Junk, 1966).

9   O. Shimamura, *Bioluminescence: Chemical Principles and Methods* (Singapore: World Scientific, 2006). The biographical detail that I mention here evokes a harrowing story by A. Nosaka, *La Tombe des lucioles* (1967), translated to French by P. De Vos (Arles: Philippe Picquier, 1995), 19–67: a story in which Nosaka gives "fireflies" a spelling that literally means "fire that falls drop by drop" and in which the insects' small lights form the counterpoint—discreet but stubborn—of incendiary bombs, of tracer ammunition, that is, of the moving dust that passed above the Japanese cities bombarded in 1945.

10   There are examples of fireflies (dried out, dark) captured in amber in the work of D. Grimaldi and M. S. Engel, *Evolution of Insects* (Cambridge: Cambridge University Press, 2005), 374–86.

11   Gilles Deleuze and Félix Guattari, *Kafka: Towards a Minor Literature,* trans. Dana Polan (Minneapolis: University of Minnesota Press, 1986), 16–17.

12   Pier Paolo Pasolini, "La veille," trans. to French by A. Bouleau and S. Bevacqua, *Cahiers du cinéma,* no. 9 (1981): 18.

13   Pasolini, "Le génocide," 266. One could doubtless analyze this position according to what Franco Fortini named, beginning in 1959, "contradiction" at work in Pasolini. See F. Fortini, "La contradizione," in *Attraverso Pasolini* (Turin: Einauldi, 1993),

21–37, and Fortini, "Pasolini politico," in *Attraverso Pasolini*, 191–206.

14   Jean-François Lyotard, *Libidinal Economy,* trans. Iain Hamilton Grant (London: Continuum, 2004).

15   Michel Foucault, *The History of Sexuality, Vol. 1: An Introduction,* trans. Robert Hurley (New York: Vintage, 1990).

16   See Dominique Champiat, "La Bioluminescence," in *Bio-chimiluminescence,* ed. D. Champiat and J.-P. Larpent (Paris: Masson, 1993), 15: "The function of a light signal that would seem the most obvious is to illuminate. Paradoxically, there exist only a few non-ambiguous examples of this role." No case of this type is attested among fireflies.

17   Champiat, 30.

18   Claude Gudin, *Une histoire naturelle de la séduction* (Paris: Seuil, 2003), 36–37. On the biochemistry of this "firefly system," see Champiat, "La Bioluminescence," 34–58 ("The firefly system: benzothiazole-type luciferene, oxidation preceded by activation of the substrate"). See also J. F. Case, P. J. Herring, B. H. Robison, S. H. D. Haddock, L. J. Kricka, and P. E. Stanley, eds., "Firefly Bioluminescence," in *Proceedings of the 11th International Symposium on Bioluminescence and Chemiluminescence* (Singapore: World Scientific, 2001), 143–204. On debates concerning the origins of bioluminescence—adaptationist interpretation versus phylogenetic interpretation—see David Grimaldi and Michael Engel, *Evolution of the Insects* (Cambridge: Cambridge University Press, 2005), 383–87.

19   Adolf Portmann, "L'autoprésentation, motif de l'élaboration des formes vivantes," trans. to French by J. Dewitte, *Études phénoménologiques* 12, no. 23–24 (1996): 131–64. Also, in general, Adolf Portmann, *Animal Forms and Patterns: A Study of the Appearance of Animals,* trans. Hella Czech (New York: Schocken Books, 1967). On Portmann's work, see G. Thinès, "La forme animale selon Buytendijk et Portmann," *Études*

phénoménologiques 12, no. 23–24 (1996): 195–207; "Animalité et humanité: autour d'Adolf Portmann" (special issue), *Revue européenne des sciences* 27, no. 115 (1999).

20 J. E. Lloyd, "Bioluminescence and Communication in Insects," *Annual Review of Entomology* 28 (1983): 131–60; M. A. Branham and J. W. Wenzel, "The Origin of Photic Behavior and the Evolution of Sexual Communication in Fireflies," *Cladistics* 19 (2003): 1–22.

21 See J.-J. Chang, J. Fisch, and F.-A. Popp, eds., *Biophotons* (Dordrecht, Netherlands: Kluwer Academic, 1998).

22 One may here again recognize the very definition of the "dialectical image"; see Walter Benjamin, "Paris, Capital of the Nineteenth Century" (exposé of 1935), in *Arcades Project,* 4–5. [See also N. Convolute, "On the Theory of Knowledge, Theory of Progress," in *Arcades Project,* 461–63.—T.N.] A concept that henceforth must be confronted with Ernst Bloch's concept of "wishful images" in *The Principle of Hope,* trans. Neville Plaice, Stephen Plaice, and Paul Knight (Cambridge, Mass.: MIT Press, 1995).

23 Hannah Arendt, "Imagination," in *Lectures on Kant's Political Philosophy,* trans. Ronald Beiner, 79–89 (Chicago: University of Chicago Press, 1992).

24 Jacques Rancière, *The Politics of Aesthetics: The Distribution of the Sensible,* trans. Gabriel Rockhill (London: Bloomsbury, 2004); Rancière, *The Future of the Image,* trans. Gregory Elliott (Brooklyn, N.Y.: Verso, 2007); Rancière, *The Emancipated Spectator,* trans. Gregory Elliott (Brooklyn, N.Y.: Verso, 2009).

25 See Stéphane Mosès, *The Angel of History: Rosenzweig, Benjamin, Scholem,* trans. Barbara Harshay (Stanford, Calif.: Stanford University Press, 2008); Michael Löwy, *Fire Alarm: Reading Walter Benjamin "On the Concept of History,"* trans. Chris Turner (London: Verso, 2005); Georges Didi-Huberman, *Ce que nous voyons, ce qui nous regarde* (Paris: Minuit, 1992);

Didi-Huberman, *Devant le temps* (Paris: Minuit, 2000).

26 Aby Warburg, "Pagan-Antique Prophecy in Words and Images in the Age of Luther," in *The Renewal of Pagan Antiquity: Contributions to the Cultural History of the European Renaissance,* trans. David Britt, 598–667 (Los Angeles, Calif.: Getty Research Institute, 1999). On the idea of survivals, see Georges Didi-Huberman, *The Surviving Image: Phantoms of Time and Time of Phantoms: Aby Warburg's Art History,* trans. Harvey Mendelsohn (University Park: Pennsylvania State University Press, 2016). On the political dimension of Warburgian iconology, see Charlotte Schoell-Glass, *Aby Warburg and Anti-Semitism: Political Perspectives on Image and Culture,* trans. Samuel Pakucs-Willcocks (Detroit, Mich.: Wayne State University Press, 2008).

27 Ernesto de Martino, *Morte e pianto rituale: dal lamento funebre al pianto di Maria* (Torino: Bollati Boringhieri, 2000); also Martino, *La Fin du monde: essai sur les apocalypses culturelles,* trans. to French by Giordana Charuty (Paris: EHESS, 2016).

28 *La Ricotta,* dir. Pier Paolo Pasolini, in *Ro.Go.Pa.G.* (Italy: Arco Film, 1963).

3. Apocalypses?

1 Giorgio Agamben, "Aby Warburg and the Nameless Science," in *Potentialities,* trans. Daniel Heller-Roazen, 89–103 (Stanford, Calif.: Stanford University Press, 1999).

2 Giorgio Agamben, *Stanzas: Word and Phantasm in Western Culture,* trans. Ronald L. Martinez (Minneapolis: University of Minnesota Press, 1993). Benjamin mentions the "documentary project on 'Fantasy'" in his *Moscow Diary,* trans. Richard Sieburth (Cambridge, Mass.: Harvard University Press, 1986), 101.

3 Giorgio Agamben, *The Signature of All Things: On Method,* trans. Luca D'Isanto (Brooklyn, N.Y.: Zone Books, 2010), 18, 107.

4 Giorgio Agamben, "What Is the Contemporary?," in *"What*

Is an Apparatus?" and Other Essays, trans. David Kishik and Stefan Pedatella (Stanford, Calif.: Stanford University Press, 2009), 41.

5   Agamben, 46.

6   Agamben, 41–46.

7   Agamben, 51.

8   Agamben, 52.

9   Giorgio Agamben, "What Is a People?," in *Means without End,* trans. Vincenzo Binetti and Cesare Casarino, 29–36 (Minneapolis: University of Minnesota Press, 2000); Agamben, "Languages and Peoples," in *Means without End,* 63–72.

10   Giorgio Agamben, "Le corps à venir: Lire ce qui n'a jamais été écrit," in *Image et mémoire,* 113–19 (Paris: Desclée de Brouwer, 2004).

11   Giorgio Agamben, "For an Ethics of the Cinema," trans. John V. Garner and Colin Williamson, in *Cinema and Agamben: Ethics, Biopolitics and the Moving Image,* ed. Henrik Gustafsson and Asbjørn Grønstad, 19–54 (New York: Bloomsbury, 2014); Agamben, *The Coming Community,* trans. Michael Hardt (Minneapolis: University of Minnesota Press, 1993); Agamben, "The Face," in *Means without End,* 91–99.

12   Giorgio Agamben, *Infancy and History: On the Destruction of Experience,* trans. Liz Heron (New York: Verso, 2007).

13   Agamben, 15.

14   Walter Benjamin, "The Storyteller: Observations on the Works of Nicolai Leskov," trans. Harry Zohn, in *Selected Writings,* ed. Michael Jennings (Cambridge, Mass.: Belknap Press of Harvard University Press, 2002), 3:143–44; see also Benjamin, "Experience and Poverty," trans. Rodney Livingstone, in *Selected Writings,* ed. Michael Jennings et al., 2:731–37 (Cambridge, Mass.: Belknap Press of Harvard University Press, 1999).

15   Agamben, *Infancy and History,* 16–17.

16   Agamben, 47.

17 Agamben, 58, 60, italics original.

18 Giorgio Agamben, *Remnants of Auschwitz: The Witness and the Archive,* trans. Daniel Heller-Roazen (Brooklyn, N.Y.: Zone Books, 2002), 41–53.

19 Agamben, "Notes on Gesture," in *Means without End,* 48.

20 Aristotle, *Metaphysics Z,* trans. Hugh Tredennick (Cambridge, Mass.: Harvard University Press, 1933), 1029a–1030b. See also the classic analysis of these passages by P. Aubenque, *Le probleme de l'être chez Aristote* (Paris: Presses universitaires de France, 1962).

21 Immanuel Kant, "On a Newly Arisen Superior Tone in Philosophy," trans. Peter Fenves, in *Raising the Tone of Philosophy: Late Essays by Immanuel Kant, Transformative Critique by Jacques Derrida,* ed. Peter Fenves, 51–82 (Baltimore: Johns Hopkins University Press, 1993).

22 Jacques Derrida, "On a Newly Arisen Apocalyptic Tone in Philosophy," trans. John P. Leavey Jr., in Fenves, *Raising the Tone of Philosophy,* 147–48, 151, and 157.

23 Derrida, 157.

24 Derrida, 127–28.

25 Derrida, 165–67. Significantly, Agamben himself articulates his "apocalyptic experience" in a reflection on voice in *Infancy and History,* 7–15.

26 Derrida, 167.

27 Adorno, *Metaphysics: Concepts and Problems,* trans. Rolf Tiedemann (Stanford, Calif.: Stanford University Press, 2002), 107.

28 On the distinction between tradition and survival, an important one, see Georges Didi-Huberman, "The Surviving Image: Aby Warburg and Tylorian Anthropology," trans. Vivian Sky Rehberg, *Oxford Art Journal* 25, no. 1 (2002): 61–69.

29 Agamben, *Remnants of Auschwitz*; also Agamben, *The Time That Remains: A Commentary on the Letter to the Romans,* trans. Patricia Dailey (Stanford, Calif.: Stanford University Press, 2005).

30 Warburg, "Pagan-Antique Prophecy."

31 Agamben, *Time That Remains*, 145.

32 Agamben, *The Kingdom and the Glory: For a Genealogy of Economy and Government*, trans. Lorenzo Chiesa (Stanford, Calif.: Stanford University Press, 2011).

33 But also Hermann Cohen, Martin Buber, Gershom Scholem, Ernst Bloch, Hans Jonas, Leo Strauss, or Emmanuel Levinas. Regarding messianism in their works, one may read P. Bouretz's wide synthesis *Witnesses for the Future: Philosophy and Messianism*, trans. Michael B. Smith (Baltimore: Johns Hopkins University Press, 2010).

34 Stéphane Mosès, "Messianisme du temps présent," *Lignes* 27 (2008): 35.

35 Walter Benjamin, "On the Concept of History," trans. Harry Zohn, in *Selected Writings, 1938–1940* (Cambridge, Mass.: Belknap Press of Harvard University Press, 2006), 4:397.

36 See D. Cohen-Levinas, "Le temps de la fêlure," *Lignes* 27 (2008): 5–8, or Cohen-Levinas, "Temps contre temps: Le messianisme de l'autre," *Lignes* 27 (2008): 79–92.

37 Jacques Derrida, "Force of Law: The Mystical Foundation of Authority," trans. Mary Quaintance, in *Deconstruction and the Possibility of Justice*, ed. Drucilla Cornell and Michael Rosenfeld (New York: Routledge, 1992), 26.

38 See, e.g., the works collected in Agamben's *Image et mémoire: écrits sur l'image, la danse, et le cinéma*; or in Giorgio Agamben, *Profanations*, trans. Jeff Fort (Brooklyn, N.Y.: Zone Books, 2015).

39 Agamben, *Kingdom and the Glory*, 68–105.

40 Agamben, 197–252.

4. Peoples

1 Agamben, *Kingdom and the Glory*, 64.

2 Giorgio Agamben, *State of Exception*, trans. Kevin Attell (Chicago: University of Chicago Press, 2005).

3   Carl Schmitt, *State, Movement, People: The Triadic Structure of the Political Unity; the Question of Legality*, trans. Simona Draghici (Corvallis, Oreg.: Plutarch Press, 2001).

4   Benjamin, "On the Concept of History," 392.

5   Jacob Taubes, *Occidental Eschatology*, trans. David Ratmoko (Stanford, Calif.: Stanford University Press, 2009); Taubes, *The Political Theology of Paul*, trans. Aleida Assmann (Stanford, Calif.: Stanford University Press, 2004).

6   Jacob Taubes, *To Carl Schmitt: Letters and Reflections*, trans. Keith Tribe (New York: Columbia University Press, 2013), 55.

7   Taubes, 27: "Simply as an arch-Jew I hesitate to burn my bridges. Because in all the unspeakable horror we were spared one thing. We had no choice: Hitler made us into absolute enemies. And there was no choice in this, nor any judgment, certainly not about others." And "So I said to myself: Listen, Jacob, you are not the judge, as a Jew especially you are not the judge" (52). See also Raphael Gross's study *Carl Schmitt and the Jews: The "Jewish Question," the Holocaust, and German Legal Theory*, trans. Joel Golb (Madison: University of Wisconsin Press, 2007).

8   Carl Schmitt, *Political Theology: Four Chapters on the Theory of Sovereignty*, trans. George Schwab (Chicago: University of Chicago Press, 2010).

9   Taubes, *To Carl Schmitt*, 54.

10 Agamben, *Kingdom and the Glory*, 75 (in reference to Schmitt, *State, Movement, People*).

11 Agamben, 68–105.

12 Agamben, 64.

13 Taubes, *To Carl Schmitt*, 17.

14 Pier Paolo Pasolini, "Mes mille et une nuits," in *Écrits sur le cinema* (Lyon: Presses universitaires de Lyon-Institut Lumière, 1987), 232–38 (a text unfortunately not included in the more recent edition of *Écrits sur le cinéma: Petits dialogues avec les*

films 1957–1974 [Paris: Cahiers du cinéma, 2000]; my thanks to Delphine Chaix for alerting me to this text).

15 Agamben, *Kingdom and the Glory*, 167–253.

16 Agamben, 253.

17 Agamben.

18 Agamben, 253–54.

19 Agamben, 254.

20 Carl Schmitt, *Constitutional Theory*, trans. Jeffrey Seitzer (Durham, N.C.: Duke University Press, 2008), 272 (cited in Agamben, *Kingdom and the Glory*, 254).

21 Schmitt, 275.

22 Agamben, *Kingdom and the Glory*, 255–56, 258.

23 Agamben, 258 (a proposition that Agamben reiterates and summarizes on p. 259).

24 See Serge Moscovici, *The Age of the Crowd: A Historical Treatise on Mass Psychology*, trans. J. C. Whitehouse (Cambridge: Cambridge University Press, 1985), and, for the dialectical countersubject, Moscovici, *Social Influence and Social Change*, trans. Carol Sherrard and Greta Heinz (London: Academic Press, 1981).

25 Schmitt, *Constitutional Theory*, 131, 271.

26 Schmitt, 302–3.

27 Schmitt, *State, Movement, People*, 52.

28 G. W. F. Hegel, *The Phenomenology of Spirit*, trans. A.V. Miller (Oxford: Oxford University Press, 1977), 1:128.

29 See Michael Hardt and Antonio Negri, *Empire* (Boston: Harvard University Press, 2000), and Hardt and Negri, *Multitude: War and Democracy in the Age of Empire* (New York: Penguin, 2004).

30 Philippe Mesnard and Claudine Mahan, *Giorgio Agamben à l'épreuve d'Auschwitz* (Paris: Kimé, 2001), 14–76; Éric Marty, "Agamben et les tâches de l'intellectuel. À propos d'État d'exception," *Les Temps modernes* 626 (2003–4): 215–33

(reworked and reprinted in *Une querelle avec Alain Badiou, philosophe* [Paris: Gallimard, 2007], 131–55).

31 Agamben, *Signature of All Things,* 9.
32 Agamben, 81–110.
33 Agamben, 99.
34 Walter Benjamin, "Excavation and Memory," trans. Rodney Livingstone, in Jennings et al., *Selected Writings,* 2:576.
35 Walter Benjamin, *Origin of German Tragic Drama,* trans. John Osborne (New York: Verso, 1998), 47.
36 Benjamin, 46.
37 Walter Benjamin, *Origine du drame baroque allemand,* trans. to French by S. Muller and A. Hirt (Paris: Flammarion, 1985), 45, and Benjamin, *Origin of German Tragic Drama,* 47. [To retain the author's connotation, I have translated from the French for the first part of this citation, regarding the dialectic as "witness to the origin," while relying on John Osbourne's translation for the remainder.—T.N.]
38 Benjamin, 45.
39 Benjamin, "Paris, Capital of the Nineteenth Century," and Benjamin, "On the Concept of History," 395.
40 Agamben, *Signature of All Things,* 18–19, 22.
41 Agamben, 24.
42 Alain Faure and Jacques Rancière, *La Parole ouvrière* (Paris: La Fabrique, 2007).

5. Destructions?

1 Walter Benjamin, "On the Concept of History," 390.
2 Benjamin, 397.
3 Benjamin, 390–91.
4 Walter Benjamin, "Sur le concept de l'histoire," in *Écrits français,* ed. J.-M. Monnoyer (Paris: Gallimard Folio, 1991), 435.
5 Walter Benjamin, "Paralipomena to 'On the Concept of History,'" trans. Edmund Jephcott and Howard Eiland, in *Selected*

Writings (Cambridge, Mass.: Belknap Press of Harvard University Press, 2006), 4:403.

6 Benjamin, "On the Concept of History," 391.

7 Benjamin, "Paralipomena," 404.

8 See Georges Didi-Huberman, "L'image brûle," in *Penser par les images: Autour des travaux de Georges Didi-Huberman,* ed. L. Zimmerman, 11–52 (Nantes, France: Cécile Defaut, 2006).

9 I use the term *recourse [ressource]* after a recent discussion with Ludger Schwarte, who comments, in this sense, on the Heideggerian term *Möglichkeit* to critique Agamben's usage, in the sense—the double sense—of "power" *(potere)*. See Schwarte, *Philosophie der Architektur* (Munich: Wilhelm Fink, 2009), 325–36. Sigrid Weigel, for his part, has long criticized Agamben's reading of Benjamin's texts on violence, the state of exception, the idea of secularization, the relationship between the martyr and the sovereign, and Agamben's usage of juridico-theological terms from the Judeo-Christian tradition. See Weigel, *Walter Benjamin: Die Kreatur, das Heilige, die Bilder* (Frankfurt-am-Main, Germany: Fischer, 2008), 57–109.

10 Benjamin, "Storyteller," 143.

11 Agamben, *Infancy and History,* 16.

12 Benjamin, "Storyteller," 143.

13 Benjamin.

14 Benjamin, 143.

15 Benjamin, 147.

16 Benjamin, 143.

17 Benjamin, 162.

18 Lucretius, *De la nature,* 216–50.

19 Benjamin, *Origin of German Tragic Drama,* 55, 99.

20 Benjamin, "Storyteller," 149.

21 Benjamin, 154.

22 Benjamin, 157.

23 Benjamin, 148.

24   Benjamin, 146.

25   Theodor W. Adorno, "Notes on Beckett," trans. Dirk Van Hulle and Shane Weller, *Journal of Beckett Studies* 19, no. 2 (2010): 157–78.

26   Agamben, "L'image immémoriale," in *La Puissance de la pensée,* 283–92.

27   Agamben, 290.

28   Agamben, *Infancy and History,* 16.

29   Walter Benjamin, *Images de pensée* (Paris: Christian Bourgois, 1998); Benjamin, *On Hashish,* trans. Howard Eiland (Cambridge, Mass.: Belknap Press of Harvard University Press, 2006), 58–60, 79–85.

30   Henri Michaux, "Ordeals, Exorcisms," trans. David Ball, in *Darkness Moves: An Henri Michaux Anthology* (Berkeley: University of California Press, 1994), 84.

31   René Char, *Hypnos: Notes from the French Resistance, 1943–1944,* trans. Mark Hutchinson (Calcutta: Seagull Books, 2014), 171–233.

32   Victor Klemperer, *LTI, the Language of the Third Reich: A Philologist's Notebook,* trans. Martin Brady (London: Continuum, 2006), 8.

33   See Emanuel Ringelblum, *Notes from the Warsaw Ghetto,* trans. Jacob Sloan (Shelter Island Heights, N.Y.: iBooks, 2015); Hillel Seidman, *Warsaw Ghetto Diaries,* trans. Yosef Israel (Jerusalem: Targum Press, 1997); Ber Mark and Isaiah Avrech, eds., *The Scrolls of Auschwitz* (Tel Aviv: Am Oved, 1985).

34   See Georges Didi-Huberman, *Images in Spite of All,* trans. Shane B. Lillis (Chicago: University of Chicago Press, 2008).

35   Benjamin, "Storyteller," 151–53. It is doubtless necessary to link this "authority of the dying" to the theme of the "weak messianic force" in Benjamin, of which we find echoes in the work of Jacques Derrida. On this last, see the work of L. Odello, *Écritures du politique: À partir de Jacques Derrida,* of which a

chapter is titled, "L'im-pouvoir de la souveraineté (ou force faible)." This is Odello's thesis, defended at the University of Trieste in 2007.

6. Images

1   Benjamin, "Storyteller," 154.
2   Hana Volavková, ed., *"I Never Saw Another Butterfly . . .": Children's Drawings and Poems from Terezin Concentration Camp, 1942–1944*, exp. 2nd ed. (New York: Schocken Books, 1994), vi, 185.
3   Charlotte Beradt, "Dreams under Dictatorship," *Free World* 6, no. 4 (1943): 333.
4   Benjamin, "Storyteller," 156–57.
5   Charlotte Beradt, *The Third Reich of Dreams*, trans. Adriane Gottwald (Chicago: Quadrangle Books, 1968), 9.
6   Beradt, 31.
7   Beradt, 53.
8   Beradt, 135. [The note in brackets is Beradt's.—T.N.]
9   Beradt, 100.
10 Reinhart Koselleck, "Afterword to Charlotte Beradt's *The Third Reich of Dreams*," in *The Practice of Conceptual History*, trans. Todd Samuel Presner (Stanford, Calif.: Stanford University Press, 2002), 333.
11 Koselleck, 334.
12 Koselleck, 335.
13 Koselleck, 337.
14 Koselleck, 328.
15 Pierre Fédida, *Crise et contre-transfert* (Paris: Presses universitaires de France, 1992), 37, 44.
16 Georges Bataille, *On Nietzsche: The Will to Chance,* trans. Stuart Kendall (Albany: SUNY Press, 2015), 137, italics original.
17 Georges Bataille, *Guilty,* trans. Stuart Kendall (Albany: SUNY Press, 2011), 9.

18   Bataille, 19.

19   Georges Bataille, *Inner Experience*, trans. Leslie Anne Boldt (Albany: SUNY Press, 1988).

20   Georges Bataille, "Madame Edwarda," in *"My Mother," "Madame Edwarda," "The Dead Man,"* trans. Austryn Wainhouse (London: Marion Moyars, 1989), 148–59.

21   Georges Bataille, "Socratic College," trans. Michelle Kendall and Stuart Kendall, in *The Unfinished System of Nonknowledge*, ed. Stuart Kendall (Minneapolis: University of Minnesota Press, 2001), 12.

22   Michel Surya, *Georges Bataille: An Intellectual Biography*, trans. Krzysztof Fijalkowski and Michael Richardson (New York: Verso, 2002), 318.

23   Georges Bataille, "The Dead Man," in *"My Mother," "Madame Edwarda," "The Dead Man,"* 167.

24   Bataille, *Guilty*, 113.

25   Bataille, *Inner Experience*, 7.

26   Bataille, 9, 40.

27   Bataille, 12.

28   Bataille, 59.

29   Bataille, 50.

30   Bataille, 84, 95, 127.

31   Bataille, 124.

32   Bataille, 13.

33   Bataille, *On Nietzsche*, 7.

34   Bataille, 59–162.

35   Bataille, 165–68.

36   Bataille, 3.

37   Bataille, 41. [Italics in original.—T.N.]

38   Bataille, 94.

39   See Surya, *Georges Bataille*, 365–67.

40   Georges Bataille, "A propos de *Pour qui sonne le glas* d'Ernest Hemingway," in *Georges Bataille: Une liberté souveraine*, ed.

Michel Surya, 41–47 (Paris: Fourbis, 1997) (I prefer this edition because the version in the *Œuvres complètes* is truncated). On this admirable text, see also Georges Didi-Huberman, "L'œil de l'expérience," in *Vivre le sens,* 147–77 (Paris: Le Seuil-Centre Roland Barthes, 2008).

41   Agamben, *Coming Community,* 1–2, 17–20.

42   Agamben, 39–56.

43   Maurice Blanchot, *The Infinite Conversation,* trans. Susan Hanson (Minneapolis: University of Minnesota Press, 1993), 130.

44   Blanchot, 134, 135.

45   Hannah Arendt, "On Humanity in Dark Times: Thoughts on Lessing," trans. Clara Winston and Richard Winston, in *Men in Dark Times* (New York: Harcourt, Brace, 1968), 4.

46   Arendt.

47   Arendt, 5, 9, emphasis mine.

48   Arendt, 21.

49   Arendt, 23.

50   Hannah Arendt, "The Gap between Past and Present," in *Between Past and Future: Eight Exercises in Political Thought* (New York: Penguin, 2006), 4.

51   Arendt, 10.

52   Arendt, 11–12.

53   Sigmund Freud, *The Interpretation of Dreams,* trans. A. A. Brill (New York: Macmillan, 1913), 493.

54   By contrast, the choice of Eisenstein for his cinema on the history of peoples. See Sergei Eisenstein, *Beyond the Stars: The Memoirs,* trans. William Powell (London: British Film Institute, 1995).

55   Laura Waddington, *Border* (Lovestreams Productions, 2004). See also Georges Didi-Huberman, "Figurants," in *Dictionnaire mondial des images,* ed. L. Gervereau (Paris: Nouveau Monde, 2006), 398–400.

Georges Didi-Huberman is lecturer at the École des hautes études en sciences sociales in Paris and professor of art history and philosophy at the European Graduate School (EGS) in Saas-Fee, Switzerland. He is the author of *Being a Skull: Place, Contact, Thought, Sculpture* (Univocal, Minnesota, 2016).

Lia Swope Mitchell is a writer and translator in Minneapolis. She is completing her PhD in French at the University of Minnesota.